ARGUING WITH PEOPLE

ARGUING WITH PEOPLE

MICHAEL A. GILBERT

broadview press

LIBRARY AND ARCHIVES CANADA CATALOGUING IN PUBLICATION

Gilbert, Michael A., author
   Arguing with people / Michael A. Gilbert.

Includes bibliographical references and index.
ISBN 978-1-55481-170-0 (pbk.)

   1. Persuasion (Rhetoric). 2. Debates and debating. I. Title.

P301.5.P47G54 2014   808   C2014-901752-9

BROADVIEW PRESS is an independent, international publishing house, incorporated in 1985.

We welcome comments and suggestions regarding any aspect of our publications—please feel free to contact us at the addresses below or at broadview@broadviewpress.com.

NORTH AMERICA
Post Office Box 1243
Peterborough, Ontario
K9J 7H5 Canada

customerservice@broadviewpress.com

555 Riverwalk Parkway
Tonawanda, NY 14150, USA
TEL: (705) 743-8990
FAX: (705) 743-8353

UK, EUROPE, CENTRAL ASIA, MIDDLE EAST, AFRICA, INDIA, AND SOUTHEAST ASIA
Eurospan Group, 3 Henrietta St., London WC2E 8LU, United Kingdom
TEL: 44 (0) 1767 604972 FAX: 44 (0) 1767 601640
eurospan@turpin-distribution.com

AUSTRALIA AND NEW ZEALAND
NewSouth Books
c/o TL Distribution, 15-23 Helles Ave.
Moorebank, NSW 2170, Australia
TEL: (02) 8778 9999 FAX: (02) 8778 9944
orders@tldistribution.com.au

www.broadviewpress.com

Broadview Press acknowledges the financial support of the Government of Canada through the Canada Book Fund for our publishing activities.

Edited by Robert M. Martin
Typesetting by Em Dash Design

Printed in Canada

For my Queen, Diane Guité Gilbert
and
my Princess, Emma Alison Wymant

Only the existence of an argumentation that is neither
compelling nor arbitrary
can give meaning to human freedom,
a state in which a reasonable choice can be exercised.
(Perelman and Olbrechts-Tyteca 1969, 514)

CONTENTS

ACKNOWLEDGMENTS

This book is a work of piracy. I have pirated ideas from some of the brightest and best minds I have come across in my more than 40 years of academic work. If there is good to be found in here, it is to their credit. If there is not, then it due to my inability to successfully communicate their insights. While the list of those whose work has influenced me is very long, I want to single out a few who had a major impact. I want to thank, first and foremost, Charlie Willard who encouraged me to step back into the conference realm when earlier experiences had soured me. I also want to thank Ralph Johnson and Tony Blair who embraced me as a colleague even when they disagreed—which was often. Frans van Eemeren and the late Rob Grootendorst tolerated my critique of their wonderful work when it was, for me, a way of finding my own way. Gratitude also goes to Christopher Tindale, Leo Groarke, Hans Hansen, Dale Hample, Harvey Siegel, Sharon Bailin, Claudio Duran, Daniel Cohen, David Godden, Chris Reed, and many others.

I want to extend my appreciation to my department at York University, as well as the University itself for specific funding and release time to help me write. I also benefitted greatly from a Social Sciences and Humanities Research Council Standard Grant which allowed me to travel and attend many valuable conferences. My students at York, especially those in my fourth year seminars over the past several years read drafts of the manuscript and often had thoughtful and helpful suggestions: thank you all. The reviewers Broadview Press used both in the early stages of the proposal and later of the manuscript were careful, thoughtful and provided me with many worthwhile suggestions and insights. This is also true of Bob Martin who did the final edits with patience and understanding. Thanks, of course, goes to Stephen Latta, Philosophy Editor at Broadview, who saw the value and uniqueness of this project.

Many of my friends helped me by reading the manuscript as well as holding my hand in times of stress and doubt. Thanks go to all the Goofy Guys: Alan, Alex, Andrew, Mike, Peter, and Simon my grammarian. I thank Jack Malick for being there for me, and especially Dodie Richman who had the unenviable job of being my wailing wall, a task she managed with affection and finesse.

Above all I want to thank my beloved Diane, my queen who had to put up with my absentmindedness and anxieties in addition to being a reader and sounding board. Alongside her was my princess Emma who also suffered through the process. Without them I could not have done it, and probably would not have wanted to.

A writer is often asked, How long did it take you to write the book? While my answer changes, it is always the same. In this case, the answer is 68 years, and thanks to all who helped along the way.

Michael A. Gilbert

INTRODUCTION

The Critical Reasoning course you take in your college or university, in training sessions and workshops, is probably the single most important and useful course you will encounter. In my 40 years of university teaching, students who get back to me to say "hi" invariably mention the Critical Reasoning course they took from me as the most useful and pertinent course in their post-secondary education. This book is addressed to two audiences. On the one hand, it is intended as extra or background reading in a Critical Thinking or Critical Reasoning course. But on the other, I also want to make the developments and advances of contemporary Argumentation Theory available to the many people whose occupations and interests involve them in argumentation on a daily basis. In sum, this book is intended for anyone interested in improving and extending their argument skills.

Critical Thinking courses, by whatever name, inform you of essential information for making your way through life. The ability to recognize arguments and argument structure, to understand the concept of validity, to appreciate how to evaluate argument strength, are all skills that you will use in every career and in every aspect of your life. The reason is simple: we constantly move forward through disagreement, controversy, discussion, and decision making—we are *always* arguing, discussing, clarifying, disagreeing, exploring, testing, wondering, and generally trying to make sense of a dense and confusing world. For these very straightforward reasons, Critical Thinking is a vital subject.

This book is *not* a Critical Reasoning textbook, but is the next important step in becoming accomplished and skilled in understanding and navigating disagreement. It is meant to fill in the gaps left by a traditional Critical Reasoning course by introducing material that has been developed over the last 50 years in the field known as Argumentation Theory. This field is interdisciplinary, drawing primarily from Informal Logic, Critical Thinking, Linguistics, Discourse Analysis, Communication Theory, Rhetoric, and Social Psychology.

The essential difference between Argumentation Theory and traditional Critical Thinking is that Argumentation Theory concerns itself with disagreement and argument as it takes place between *real people in real situations*. Critical Thinking, with its focus on argument structure and evaluation, of necessity draws its examples and objects of study from static and non-interactive arguments such as editorials, letters to the editor, and essays. Examining these and applying Critical Thinking rules and assessments to them is a crucial component in increasing your argument awareness. You will spend a great deal of time over the years reading arguments and listening to speeches and deciding whether to accept or reject them. Nonetheless, I am convinced that dialogic arguments, that is, arguments that take place between people, is where most of our opinions are formed and molded. Certainly there are examples of dialogic arguments in Critical Thinking that appear in a number of texts, but it is difficult to create the kind of situation amenable to the application of rules and analysis Critical Thinking requires.

Working with and understanding real arguments—disputes occurring on the hoof—requires an approach that includes but goes beyond Critical Thinking texts. Most of the exercises in this book, for instance, are semi-structured interactions with a partner. In other words, to learn how to understand and manage active arguments, you must undertake them. The difference is that you will be paying particular attention to certain aspects during the course of the discussion. These exercises are not easy, as you will have to be a participant and an observer at the same time. Reports that you submit on these exercises can be judged on the attention paid to the arguments you created, the extent to which you listened and understood your partner's arguments, your awareness of the Critical Thinking rules and assessments at play, and your analysis of how the rules and guidelines presented here are followed.

This book is in several parts. Part 1 concerns itself with what arguments are, what kind there are, and how we need to adjust our goals and expectations depending on these factors. You already know about premises and conclusions and argument schemes—all of which are important. But you probably haven't been schooled in the difference between logical and emotional arguments, or the distinction between clinical and chaotic arguments. Part 1 will introduce a number of ideas and techniques that are basic to Argumentation Theory, so that you can take advantage of them.

In Part 2, we discuss whom we argue with and what difference the participants, location and context makes to our process. We all know people who love to argue and people who avoid it like the plague, but you need to know what these characteristics mean and how they should and do impact the way in which an argument can proceed. In this section you will become familiar with the roles that power, relationship, gender, and other personal and physical factors play in interactive communication.

Finally, in Part 3, you will learn about how to argue and how to determine the rules that are at play. You will become familiar with argument techniques and styles and what rules and conventions control it. In Part 3 we take what preceded us in Parts 1 and 2 and see how it can guide us in how to proceed in a particular argument.

Whenever you study a subject, whether it's managerial systems, auto repair, or French grammar you need to simplify it and make a manageable model you can analyze, take apart and examine. The model is made in order to understand the reality it represents, but it is essential to remember that the model is just that—a simplification, and the whole is richer and more complex. Here too, it's important to understand that while this book is broken into three sections, argumentation is not. When you argue, everything is happening at once, and trying to keep track of it all is no small feat. When you argue you need to reason, assess argument strength, premise relevance and acceptability, track goals, be sensitive to emotions, stay in the present, and listen carefully all at the same time. This can take a great deal of mental energy, so it is no wonder it can be exhausting.

Remember too that when we talk about argument we are referring to all kinds. As I explained in my book *How to Win an Argument*, "An argument is any disagreement—from the most polite discussion to the loudest brawl." In Canadian and American cultures the term 'argument' is often used to indicate something negative, while the term 'discussion' connotes something positive. There will be times when we do care about the emotional tenor of our disagreements, but when discussing arguments in general, the intention is to cover all of them regardless of how calm or emotional they are. It's also worth noting that argument style varies greatly from culture to culture. For some cultures any disagreement is considered rude and to be avoided, while in others disagreeing and arguing vehemently is a normal way of life. It's worth paying attention to this when considering the context of an argument.

A last word before we jump into argumentation with both feet. This book draws heavily on the work of many recent investigators in Argumentation Theory. Some will be mentioned by name and key points of their theories included in our study, while other scholars' work may not be directly identified. It is important to understand that all of the scholars in Argumentation Theory have made contributions that have led us to the point where an undertaking like *Arguing with People* can be attempted. Scholarship and discovery are never a function of just a few minds, but the result of a multitude of contributions, proddings, corrections, debates and the sharing of intellectual insights. All the scholars in the field have made the march forward of Argumentation Theory the success that I believe it has become. Finally, let me point out that some, perhaps many claims I make here may be controversial and not all Argumentation Theory scholars would agree with me. I do take a particular approach, and the scope of this book will not allow me to always provide all sides and all views. What you read here and, I hope, what you learn here, is my theory and I alone am responsible for any weaknesses or errors. There are other views than mine and for that I hope you go to the further readings in the appendix.

Finally, if you want to learn more about Critical Thinking, do look at my book *How to Win an Argument* published by University

Press of America—it's easy and fun. If you want more about Argumentation Theory, then read *Coalescent Argumentation* published by Lawrence Erlbaum; it's harder but manageable.

1

ALL ABOUT ARGUMENTS

In this part you will become familiar with the wide range that argument covers and how broadly the word is used. You will see that arguments unfold in stages, and that it is important to be aware of the stage you are in. Different kinds of arguments, you will see, require different attitudes and need different approaches. Finally the difference between arguing, speech making and those times when you simply cannot react will be discussed.

1.1 ABOUT ARGUMENTS

The word "argument" is an extremely rich term in the English language. It covers a wide range of communicative interactions many of which may have little in common. We'll get to that shortly, but first there's a very basic differentiation we need to make. We need to distinguish between *an argument* which is a thing, an object, or, as we will say, a *product*, and an argument as an interaction, a dynamic exchange between two or more people, which we will call a *process*. When you consider argument as a product you treat it as something that you can examine, take apart; an object that typically has components such as reasons (or premises) and a claim (or conclusion). In this sense an argument is an artifact, something that may be used in different circumstances and with different people.

Examples of arguments as products abound, including the first example here, probably the most famous argument of all time.

[1] All men are mortal; Socrates is a man; therefore Socrates is mortal.
[2] "Do you want fish for dinner tonight?"
"No. We had fish last night, and I don't want it two nights in a row."
[3] "Don't take the Peace Bridge. At this time of day it's really crowded and will take forever."

Each of these is an easily identifiable product. So you can see that being an argument that is a product does not mean it is going to be highly stilted or formal. Products are also very often incomplete, a form of argument usually called an *enthymeme*, which is a fancy name for an argument that has a missing premise or conclusion. For instance, example [2] just above, might well have been expressed without making the conclusion explicit:

[2a] "Do you want fish for dinner tonight?"
"We had fish last night."

In [2a] the claim is left implicit as it is in many arguments. So, one use of the term 'argument' is as a set of reasons and a conclusion, whether explicit or not.

—ww—

When we say "the argument," or, "that's a strong argument," or, "that argument won't stand up to scrutiny," we are probably talking about product; but sometimes we express what we mean by saying, "they had a good argument," or, "Carole and Juan had a really bad argument last night." When we speak this way we mean that people were "having an argument." This is the sense in which argument is a *process*. It is a process that takes place between people who are concerned with a disagreement. This idea of argument as both product and process was introduced by the Communication Theorist Joseph Wenzel (1979), and we will examine his ideas carefully and use them throughout.

Daniel O'Keefe (O'Keefe 1977) introduced a useful way to indicate this difference using numbers: An argument$_1$ is a product; while an argument$_2$ is a process. An argument$_2$ likely contains arguments$_1$ as objects: people who are in the process of arguing offer each other arguments. So one person makes an argument$_1$, and two people have an argument$_2$. (Get it? argument$_1$ is 1 person, argument$_2$ is 2 people.)

This distinction is important because it helps avoid confusion when we are discussing the nature of arguments. An argument$_1$, for example, typically has one or more reasons leading to an individual claim. An argument$_2$, on the other hand, may involve many claims and many reasons, and may or may not be focused on a single overriding claim.

Usually in what follows, we will mean an argument$_2$, but if it isn't clear from the context we will use O'Keefe's language to clarify.

—ɱ—

Wenzel claimed that there were three different perspectives. Argument, he said, can be understood in the sense of logic where arguments are all products, arguments$_1$, i.e., objects that can be inspected for just how they follow logical rules and how they hang together.

Wenzel pointed out that there is a second perspective: arguments can also be understood as communications that follow certain procedures, that adhere to a set of rules designed to ensure that the argument goes smoothly and fairly. This, he said, is the realm of *dialectic*. Dialectic is the study of arguments$_2$ that is geared to finding the truth or best available answer. It follows rules and *procedures* that are designed to lead to results that bring you as close to the truth as possible. Dialectical arguments are careful, precise and controlled. Unlike logic, which focuses on the structure of individual arguments$_1$ and examines them for specific logical properties, dialectic looks at arguments as they ought to occur between people. Argument partners listen to each argument, take turns and respond to what has been said. They are the sorts of arguments that Critical Thinking teachers put forward as the best examples and the models to be emulated. Alas, they don't really happen that often.

The final perspective that Wenzel introduced is that of *process*. This is the aspect of argumentation that covers such things as word choice, how arguments are presented and in what order, when and where arguments should be used, and all aspects up to and including tone of voice. This perspective, that of process, has traditionally been called *rhetoric*. While rhetoric, for many years has had a lot of bad press, within Argumentation Theory it is being re-thought and rehabilitated. Over the past 50 years scholars have been re-examining the role of rhetoric and many are finding that its reputation is unwarranted.

Much of this work has been spurred by one of the key grandfathers of modern Argumentation Theory, Chaim Perelman. His classic work was written with Mme. Lucie Olbrechts-Tyteca but was followed by many important writings he did on his own. Their work was instrumental in bringing about a new attitude toward rhetoric. Their book, *The New Rhetoric*, was originally published in French in 1958, and the English translation in 1969. Perelman and Olbrechts-Tyteca argued that all argumentation involves rhetoric, and that no matter how careful we try to be, it is impossible to avoid rhetorical choices in argumentation. They also argued that the truth is not manifest; i.e., *we can never be sure if we do or do not have the truth*. Rhetoricians care about truth, they just don't believe that we know for certain when we have it. As such, it is only argument that we can use to make decisions, resolve disputes, settle value differences, and come to the best guesses we can. While some scholars reject this attitude toward truth, others, including this author, have embraced it.

All argumentation and, really, all communication, involves rhetoric because we always make choices regarding words, inflection and so on. For example, Nuri wants to see the new romantic comedy and tells Jude that's her choice. Jude says, "Oh, sure, perfect choice." Notice that by just reading these words you have no idea if Jude is enthusiastic or opposed. It is only his tone and appearance that will make the message clear. The rhetorical, in other words, is necessary to explicate the meaning of the message.

More recently, this has been defended by Chris Tindale (1999, 2004), who argues that rhetoric is the actual foundation of argumentation and that all other perspectives depend on it. This is supported by Gilbert, who claims argument is governed by a naturally occurring set of rules that are socially enforced within most cultures (Gilbert 2007). The problem with rhetoric has always been that it appears to be focused on persuasion, rather than on getting at the truth of the matter. This is what has led to its awful reputation and means that the expression, "That's just rhetoric!" has been a way of saying that a statement sounds persuasive but is empty of any real meaning. But as Tindale and Gilbert, among others, point out, the consequences of not caring about your argument partners can be a very high price indeed. Recall the expression, "Fool me once, shame on you; fool me twice, shame on me." The point of this homily is that we are expected to pay attention to who is and who is not trustworthy, and once someone undermines our trust in them, we ought not give it back too quickly. This is actually the concept of *ethos*, a central idea in Argumentation Theory, and a topic we will return to later.

Emotion is an integral part of every argument. There is no such thing as an argument that contains no emotion at all. There is always at least some in every argument, since if there were not, then why would we be arguing in the first place? (Gilbert 1994, 2001). In other words, if you don't care about something, then why bother? Note though, (and remember in section 2.1 to reflect on this,) that the emotional push may not be about the claim, but about how you look or feel in a context: about, in other words, appearances. I may not, for example, care all that much about the truth when I disagree with your statement that Babe Ruth was the greatest ball player ever, but I may care that I look like someone who really knows his baseball stuff. I may not be arguing about the facts so much as trying to make another, rhetorical point.

Here's an example where emotion is used to advantage. In negotiating the price for an order of widgets, Natalie grudgingly allows that she will use a faster delivery method, thereby incurring higher shipment costs. In reality, she was always prepared to give in on this point but wants her negotiation partner to feel he has won something. By expressing reluctance, she is using emotion rhetorically.

Emotions play other roles as well by naturally limiting the arena or scope of argument so that we can focus on what is important. Emotions motivate arguments but are also essential in the decision-making process, and many arguments are about making decisions. Logically speaking, there are an infinite number of choices facing us when making even the simplest of decisions, but we ignore most of them without a thought by using our emotional apparatus. Think about it: when I'm on campus in Toronto and figuring out where to have lunch, I don't waste time deciding if I want to go over to Katz's Delicatessen in New York for pastrami or Fisherman's Wharf in San Francisco for fried clams. Logically those are possibilities, and they might technically qualify, but emotionally it's not an option. The fact that both would be dismissed as impractical does not speak to their status as *possible* choices. We emotionally dismiss a huge number of such possibilities without seriously considering them because our experience has taught us that they just don't feel right. The neuroscientist António Damasio (Damasio 1994) tells the story of a brain-damaged patient whose injury meant that he was unable to use or experience emotions. When the patient needed to select an alternative time for his appointment he was liable to go on forever because he did not have the emotional equipment to dismiss most of the infinite choices. So emotion keeps us from floundering in a sea of alternatives by marking them as unreasonable. When arguing it is often emotion that lets you know what is and is not relevant.

It's worth remembering that the same dynamic that allows you to make a simple decision without taking hours or days can also limit the options you take into consideration. When you want to "think outside the box," you need to let your emotions go free and take some of those "unconsidered" options and bring them back into play. This may well be one factor that is at work when we have brain-storming sessions, rely on teams, and try to shake things up by considering the unconsidered.

All this being said, there is no question that *extreme* emotion can make an argument difficult work. When emotions are very strong they can interfere, and the argument can go awry. Sometimes disputants become very angry or upset and cease listening or paying attention to the argument as a process aimed at figuring something out. When that happens, however, it does not always mean the argument is a poor one. It can mean that the most important issues have arisen, issues that are more vital than the alleged claim on the table.

Some scholars in the area of Critical Thinking and even in Argumentation Theory would have you believe that arguments are intended to be quiet and orderly discussions with careful turn-taking and great attention paid to precisely what is being said. Not only are such arguments the exception rather than the rule, but they can also hide a great deal of important information, feelings, values and ideas. I call this the *Critical-Logical* model, and in that model there is no such thing as a "hidden agenda," and the question, "I wonder what's really going on in this argument?" makes no sense. People say what they mean and mean what they say, and words and statements can be taken more or less at face value. This does makes a useful model for teaching Critical Thinking and helps you understand the basics and core concepts of arguments, but it does not really apply when arguing with people.

Clinical arguments, that is arguments with a minimum of emotion, are not always better. Sometimes clinical arguments suffer from being boring and demonstrate a lack of imagination because no one really cares. Be careful to distinguish 'clinical' from 'orderly' which will be discussed soon. Clinical means no emotional content, while orderly refers to the style of presentation. This is what distinguishes clinical from emotional.

As we move further and further along the continuum from clinical to emotional, arguments tend to become more difficult, *though not necessarily so.* Arguments between intimate partners and family, for instance, can become highly emotional, and these emotions can be important to bring out, deal with and own. Even between business partners, a highly emotional argument can often clear the air and bring out issues that otherwise might have remained hidden. So it is important not to be afraid of emotion, but rather to understand it and deal with it in effective and useful ways.

—ᴍ—

Arguments can also be distinguished in ways other than the emotional-clinical divide. That distinction identifies, more or less, the degree of emotion. Still, the way in which the argument is *conducted* is not a direct function of the emotional-logical distinction. There can be highly emotional arguments that are conducted with clarity and care, and clinical arguments that seem to make no sense at all. When it comes to the qualities of precision and comprehension, we can refer to the orderly-chaotic continuum. An argument is orderly when the dispute partners are listening to each other, taking turns, establishing their points and generally proceeding in a coherent way. So, orderly here indicates the tone of the process, whereas clinical indicates the degree of emotion. Arguments are chaotic when the partners are not listening to each other, no attention is being paid to the arguments, and there are interruptions and irrelevancies. Chaos includes shouting, making faces, mimicry, name-calling, and a host of other activities generally considered unpleasant. Do understand that there is a continuum between orderly and chaotic just as there is with clinical and emotional. Put another way, a bit of chaos, never hurt anyone and is very common in most dissensual interactions, i.e., disagreements.

We can go even further: clinical and orderly does not always equal good. Sometimes calm and highly logical arguments can lead to desperately bad results. The reason is simple. Often when emotions are left behind values do not play a sufficiently vibrant role. Morals, aesthetics, inspiration, all prevent the neglect of human considerations. When we do not take feelings, emotions, and human concerns into account, then a kind of terrible unfeeling coldness can result. This, for example, is often the basis for fascism:

draconian actions in the suppression of dissent or unrest may be very logical, but, at the same time, immoral.

—ᴍ—

Chaotic arguments can often be brought under control by requesting a summary or asking a very specific question about the position as you have best determined it. So if an argument becomes too chaotic, you can try and stabilize it. This is best done by summarizing the positions. You want to try to focus the interaction more, bring it back to the topic, so that it ceases to meander or rocket all over the place. Sometimes, when a chaotic argument is also highly emotional, perhaps involving tears and shouting, the argument has devolved into a quarrel. If that happens the best thing for you to do is to leave it and perhaps return to it later. However, even more important can be the establishment and clarification of the ground rules for the specific argument. This brings us to the next topic, the Pragma-dialectic notion of the stages of argument. Before moving on, however, one further point must be made.

In the very first section a distinction was introduced between arguments as products or artifacts (argument$_1$) and arguments as processes (argument$_2$). You may have noticed that in this current section we are considering arguments primarily as interactive processes between dispute partners. This means that the terms used are being applied to those processes as opposed to individual arguments$_1$. Yet this is not to say that within an argument$_2$ there may be individual arguments$_1$ that are emotional and some that are not. So clinical and emotional can apply to an individual argument considered as an object in an argument process, and the same is true for orderly and chaotic, though they more typically refer only to an argument$_2$. This is important for strategic reasons. An individual argument₁ should not color an entire argument, but may be used as an indicator or gauge of the larger process. This is worth remembering.

1.2 THE STAGES OF ARGUMENT

The idea of the stages of argument was first introduced by the Pragma-dialectic theorists Frans van Eemeren and the late Rob Grootendorst. The stages themselves seem very obvious, and you might wonder why you should bother paying attention to them. The stages are: confrontation, opening, argumentation, and concluding. Indeed, what could be more obvious? However, there is actually an important lesson here: you must know where you are in an argument if you are going to proceed in an intelligent and creative way. In other words, the very same reason for paying attention to the level of emotion and degree of chaos applies here. By knowing where you are in an argument, you have greater insight into how to proceed. *If you don't know where you are, you can't know where to go.*

The first stage, the confrontation stage, may seem the most obvious. Someone says something, someone else disagrees with it, and an argument starts. But a skilled reasoner always asks the question, do I want to argue? The simple presence of a disagreement does not mean an argument should automatically begin. I, for one, rarely argue about facts. If we disagree about whether or not Christmas last year fell on a Tuesday or the first day of classes in September in 2012 was the 8th, I don't see any point in arguing. We should just consult the proper authority—a calendar of the University website. Zachary says that he doesn't think that July 9th 1936 was the hottest day ever recorded in New York City. Michelle disagrees. Don't argue: research.

On the other hand, all dyed-in-the-wool Toronto Blue Jay baseball fans believe there was a triple play in the last game of the 1992 World Series. We all saw it with our own eyes. The trouble is, the umpire didn't call it, and it never made the record books (even though the umpire later admitted he missed the call—you can even search the play on YouTube and watch for yourself). So, was there a triple play or not? Suddenly, a *fact* comes into dispute, which means we end up arguing about the *kind* of evidence we accept: our own eyes, or the record book, and that is a value argument, not a fact argument. This argument, we'll call it the Triple-Play Argument, can actually have many outcomes. The variables that can influence those outcomes are interesting and will concern us shortly.

Other factors that might come into play during the confrontation stage are the various roles of those involved, e.g., are you arguing with your boss and she seems short-tempered? Is one of the dispute partners reacting in a highly emotional way? Perhaps this is best left alone? So the message here is simple: Think before you argue. Do you have a good reason to continue?

The second stage of argument is called the opening stage. It is here that the rules and procedures of the forthcoming argument are laid down. Your first reaction to this stage is probably that you never noticed it. When an argument starts, it does just that—it starts.

There's no discussion about rules or what have you. And, by and large, you're right. But that's not because there is no such stage, rather it's because you've gone through that stage before and now it is taken for granted. In other words, we don't create new rules every time we interact: so long as you are in a familiar culture you tend to just continue on.

There is, however, a "but." If something happens in the course of the discussion that is unexpected, a move, style or item of evidence not expected or usual, then you may stop the argument's process and return to the opening stage. For example, if one partner suddenly raises her voice or begins crying, the other partner might object with something like, "That's not fair!" Or, "If you're going do that I won't argue with you." When Sophie says to Jude, "I'm not going to argue with you if you keep shouting," Jude might reply, "I'm not shouting!" This exchange is actually a return to the opening stage and must be dealt with before the dispute continues.

The same thing might happen with the introduction of surprising evidence or information. Olivia says to James, "Don't tell me you never did that before. I spoke with your mother, and she says you always did that." When James replies, "You what?!? You spoke to my mother? You shouldn't have done that!" James is pulling them back into the confrontation stage where an argument will take place about whether or not Olivia has the right to talk to James's mother about James. Why the confrontation stage? Because this is a different argument. So, while they had entered the argumentation stage in the first argument, James changed the topic of the argument and yanked them back to the confrontation stage for a new one. A new topic means you begin all over again, and it pays to realize that.

Why is this important? Because it lets you know where you are. If you are not where you think you are, you can lose your way. By simply being aware that the stage of argument has changed, you can save a great deal of mis-argument. One reason why an orderly argument may become chaotic is if there is a great deal of bouncing between the stages. Imagine a discussion concerning whether or not Binney Cosmetics, a family owned mid-size business, should outsource their help line to an offshore service. The factors that enter into the discussion can range over a variety of subjects including simple economics, customer service, local job loss, public image, national loyalty, family commitments, company history, and so on and so on. The ensuing conversation has potential for bouncing all over the place. However, if attention is paid to the opening stage, it is possible to lay out parameters so that, for example, individual issues can be discussed separately. Once that has been done, the individual costs and benefits can be weighed against each other. At that time you can examine the different costs, e.g., the financial benefit of going offshore as opposed to the emotional sense of abandoning one's home country, to determine a final answer.

Being aware of this is important. Breaking an argument into its separate units, each guided by its own rules and evidence, can be very useful and focusing. When you try to do everything at once, often nothing gets done at all.

The third stage of argument is the argumentation stage, and I will actually say very little about it here since it occupies most of this book. This is where the actual argument takes place, where reasons are put forward and claims defended, objections are made and answered, and premises and conclusions tracked and followed. What we have seen so far is that the argumentation stage can bring us back to the opening stage, and even the confrontation stage. If Olivia, in the course of an argument, says to James, "Oh, that's not what I thought you meant; I have no problem with that," then they have actually leapfrogged back to the confrontation stage and agreed there is nothing to argue about. Again, the moral is to pay attention to where you are and what is going on.

—∽∽—

The final stage of argument according to the Pragma-dialecticians, is the concluding stage. This is where the argument ends or is suspended. It can end in various ways depending on the kind of argument it is. A negotiation, for example, obviously has a different kind of conclusion than an inquiry into some fact or other. An argument ends with a *resolution* to use the Pragma-dialectic term, when one of two alternatives has been accepted as correct by both disputants. Alternatively, the dispute partners can agree to settle on one answer for a variety of reasons. A *settlement* is different from a *resolution* because the former does not carry the burden of being true, while the latter does. As you will see in the next section, arguments are far more often concluded by settlement than by resolution for the very simple reason that we frequently do not have enough faith in the result to call it the truth.

Arguments also end by being suspended. Suspension can happen in many ways, and not only by a pleasant agreement to take a break. Sure, one partner may say, "You know what? This isn't getting us anywhere. Let's take a break and come back to this later."

But a suspension also occurs if one party storms away in anger or frustration, or breaks down in tears, or simply has an appointment and needs to leave. Please understand that suspensions are not bad. If the situation is not one in which a decision has to be made immediately, postponing a non-productive or upsetting dispute can be advantageous. The delay can allow information to sink in, feelings to settle down, and more information and perspectives to enter. The idea that arguments take place in a short period of time, that they begin and end in a certain serial manner is simply not true. Most decisions, where disagreement enters, are revisited and reviewed any number of times—and that is good.

1.3 KINDS OF ARGUMENT

Arguments can be looked at in different ways. They can be considered to be objects or artifacts as when we examine an argument$_1$ for its properties. You may want to poke and prod it so you can pull out the claim or conclusion, and examine the specific reasons or premises that support it. You may also be interested in the process: what rhetorical considerations come into play? You can examine the emotional commitments of the participants, their cultural and social backgrounds, as well as other information that may be relevant. Procedure is also a factor. An argument$_2$ will follow certain rules and vary from being orderly to chaotic, and it is important to pay attention to these procedural factors. In addition, you now know to pay attention to the stage of the argument you are in so that you know exactly what is at stake.

So far so good. But it turns out that not all arguments are the same, and depending on the kind of argument you are in, all the factors considered so far can have different roles and rationales.

The division of arguments into kinds goes back as far as Aristotle if not before. More recently, the prodigious philosopher and Argumentation Theorist Douglas Walton has specifically paid attention to the differences in various kinds of dialogues (Walton 1998, Walton and Krabbe 1995).

In his work he distinguishes six different kinds of arguments, but for our purposes, three will suffice. These three are *inquiry dialogue*, *negotiation*, and *persuasion dialogue*. To outrageously over-simplify, in inquiry the object is the truth; in negotiation it's to come to a mutually advantageous agreement; and in persuasion it is to instill a belief in someone. Let me quickly point out that hardly any argument is ever purely in one category or another, and that typically every argument has some elements belonging to one or the other types. Like everything else we are examining in this book, we use the categories as models and try not to confuse them with reality. Models are meant to simplify reality, not replicate it.

Inquiry, also known as "critical discussion," "dialectical reasoning," or "logical reasoning," is the Holy Grail of Critical Thinking. When involved in an inquiry, the partners are completely unattached to the outcome, desiring only to reveal the truth, or, at worst, the best possible answer to a question or best solution to a problem. When you and a dispute partner commence such an inquiry, neither of you has a pre-conceived result to which you are committed, no ego investment in the result, no advantage to be gained by one answer being deemed correct. Even when you enter the inquiry with an idea as to the proper conclusion, you have no compunction in giving it up when it has been demonstrated to be incorrect, insufficient or inadequate. Inquiries like this involve careful listening, turn taking, avoidance of strong emotion, reliance on agreed upon procedures and data, and a willingness to help your partner create a strong case. When it happens in this manner, I will call it "pure inquiry."

The difficulty is, pure inquiry almost never happens.

Before elaborating on why pure inquiry is so rare, let me first say that being rare does not mean it is impossible and certainly does not mean that it is not desirable. Two people who truly want to make a decision where they have their parameters all set, agree on them, and only want the "best" outcome can proceed in a very unattached and uncompetitive way. They might even switch sides at some point and argue just the opposite of what they were saying before. Such pure inquiry can not only happen, but can be very fulfilling and exciting as well. The point is *not* that pure inquiry does not occur, but that more often than not one or both partners is predisposed to a particular outcome or more concerned about one parameter than another.

An example will help here. Sophie and Emma own a shop that sells specialty teas as well as having a few tables to serve tea and pastries. The shop, Tea for Two, is on a street that is slowly gaining in popularity as the neighborhood around it becomes more and more gentrified. They always closed on Sunday as their business traditionally served mostly people working in the area. But now more small shops are opening up around them and the street is attracting more residents shopping or just out for a stroll. Sophie, is single and six years younger than Emma, who is married with two young children. Because of the changes in the area, Sophie is wondering if they should begin opening on Sundays. We can use this example, which we will dub the Tea for Two example, to look at the several forms of dialogue.

Since our first form of dialogue is pure inquiry, we will suppose that Emma and Sophie have no real strong feelings about whether or not they open the extra day a week. Their only concern is whether the extra cost is worth it, as they do not want to lose money by staying open. To investigate they agree to come by on several Sundays to see what the traffic is like, and if it seems substantial, then perhaps they'll open for three or four Sundays experimentally. If profits exceed costs, then they'll continue. What could be simpler?

The difficulty, which you may well have already spotted is in the simple little word "costs." In the introduction to this example I mentioned that Sophie was single but that Emma was older and had young children. This means that the cost of working on a Sunday is very likely different for each of them. Sunday, not surprisingly, is Emma's family day so her attachment to not working on that day is more than Sophie's. They might agree that they would make more money if they opened on Sundays, and that *other things being equal*, it's a good idea. But the problem from the point of view of argumentation is that other things are *never* equal. Because of this, pure inquiry is quite rare, as it requires that the dispute partners not care about the outcome and be willing to adopt whichever is best, truest, and so on. This does not mean that *inquiry* is impossible, just that *pure* inquiry is nearly so.

What I want to suggest is that inquiry can play an important role as an *intention*. That is, if you and I are facing a problem, making a decision, or trying to figure something out, we can decide to take a dialectical approach that is as close to inquiry as we can get. This allows us to take into account the reality of our situation and to put as many of the variables in play on the table. When Emma is clear that opening their shop on Sunday would be a major cost for her, she is helping steer their discussion into inquiry. This is so because it means that Sophie can take this "cost" into account, and it can be balanced along with the others.

The crucial difference between inquiry and both persuasion and negotiation is that the dispute partners are open and up front about their goals, what is at stake, and how much they care about the outcome. Caring about which position "wins" is inimical to inquiry because it hampers open discussion; it means that I am arguing strategically, and not simply investigating. Certainly on a superficial level the goals we want in negotiation and persuasion are clear: In negotiation I want as much as I can get, and in persuasion I want you to agree with me. But other, deeper or less obvious goals may well be hidden or concealed for strategic reasons. Think about the difference in the Tea for Two discussion if, at the outset, Sophie and Emma agree that, no matter what, Emma will not work on Sundays. Compare that to a discussion where Emma has not declared her feelings, but is determined that the conclusion be the one she wants. In the latter case, she will be inclined to reject every reason Sophie gives for opening on Sunday, whereas in the former they can look at them all clearly and weigh everything.

Suppose that early in the discussion Sophie says that one of her major concerns is that if they do not open on Sundays, their customers will go to different shops, and they might lose their business altogether. If Emma does not believe that Sophie understands her need to have Sunday off, she will likely reject Sophie's argument on some grounds or other. But if Emma feels that Sophie is clearly taking her goal into account, she can put her head together with Sophie and consider how likely it is that their customer loyalty might suffer.

You begin to see why I say that pure inquiry rarely exists: there are always factors that must be balanced, and as soon as these emotional or personal factors enter the argument the purity disappears. In this sense inquiry almost always has elements of negotiation in it, and do remember that an argument is rarely, if ever, strictly in one kind. That is, we are always playing one set of goals against the other. The difference is that in an inquiry all the goals are on the table, all are discussable, and *both parties are working to achieve the same goals*. Sophie accepts and respects Emma's goal of preserving her family time, and Emma understands and either shares or is interested in Sophie's concerns about the impact of not opening on Sunday. A term that is useful here is the word "heuristic." This word is from the Greek, and means "find" or "discover," and we are using it here to indicate that the persons involved in an argument are working together to discover the best answer or solution for them. We will call this kind of dialogue a *heuristic inquiry*.

In real life, heuristic inquiries are as good as we get. In a sense a heuristic inquiry is a pure inquiry that happens when you add people. The key lies in the opening stage where the discussants lay out goals and requirements for a solution. In Pragma-dialectics it states that in the opening stage the persons involved establish their roles and "their initial commitments" (Eemeren, Grootendorst, and Snoeck Henkemans 1996, 281). I want to enlarge upon this notion by expanding it to include the declaration of goals and interests. Remember, as indicated before, you can always return to the opening stage in an argument to clarify or expand on the goals that are relevant or important *as you become aware of them*. In many cases, as we will see later on, goals are not always fully known when you first enter into a discussion.

So, a heuristic inquiry involves you and your dispute partner working together to investigate an issue, solve a problem, or discover the truth. Rhetorical aspects are present but not intended to overwhelm, and the emphasis is on a high quality dialectical interaction and cooperation. You and/or your partner may feel some attachment to certain outcomes, but that attachment is on the table, available for examination and open to alternative means of satisfaction. You and your partner will use teamwork; questions and disagreement are intended to foster problem solving, not push an agenda. There should also be, I urge, awareness that heuristic inquiry is not easy. Recognizing that heuristic inquiry is not easy to maintain allows for recovery from slippage. The fact that you may have slipped from the track does not mean you cannot get back on it. Once again, awareness of what you are doing and where you are going is paramount.

—✂—

There are two main and crucial differences between heuristic inquiry and negotiation. The first is that you and your negotiation partner have different goals, and the second is that those goals are often not revealed. Unlike in a heuristic inquiry, you care first about getting what you want out of the argument and only second-arily, if at all, about what your partner in the argument gets. As a result, you will behave more strategically and not reveal how flexible your goals are and what you are willing to settle for. Of course, every negotiator and businessperson knows that the best negotiations are those where both parties end up satisfied and everyone is happy. If that happens then so much the better.

The extent to which the partners in a negotiation are open to change and are willing to alter or moderate their goals will directly impact on the process of negotiation. Sometimes, because of inex-perience, personality, or power differentials, there is little or no movement. One partner is simply demanding satisfaction of all of her demands and is unwilling to change. I call such negotiations *eristic*, which means that these negotiations are geared toward winning at all costs and have the intention of being as uncooperative as necessary. But we can conceive of a negotiation that is more heuristic than eristic: one where the partners involved want the resulting agreement to be acceptable and pleasing to all but are not, at the same time, working together toward solving a shared issue. Negotiations can range from highly eristic to highly heuristic, and the reasons for this can also vary wildly. The most important thing is to try and establish how the negotiation will proceed in the opening stage by declaring as many goals and attitudes as you are comfortable revealing.

There has been excellent work done on negotiation, including the classic and still relevant *Getting to Yes* (Fisher and Ury 1981). I want to stress, however, that a vast number of negotiations take place outside of a business context, or, if in a business context, are not about dealing with contracts, unions, and such like. Deciding where to have dinner, whether Annette should attend an outdoors camp or an arts camp, when should we replace our car, where my office should be, how easy should it be to access petty cash, are all examples of routine negotiations that will range from heuristic to eristic depending on a thousand variables. Some of these variables are basic and important and will be discussed in Part 2, but others are highly situational and impossible to pin down without analyzing the exact context.

As you will see later, it is essential to be aware of the context and the variables that come with it. This means paying attention to the needs and desires of others as well as your own. This awareness comes from practice and a commitment to knowing where you are and what's going on. It comes from paying attention to the emotional levels in an argument, the stage in which it is, what kind of dialogue it is, and exactly what is being said *and* implied.

—ᴍ—

The third type of dialogue to be mentioned is the *persuasion dialogue*. In a persuasion dialogue one of the partners in the discussion has a specific outcome in mind, be it a goal, solution, value or belief, and aims to bring the other partner in the argument around to accepting that conclusion. Toward this end the proponent, the person putting forward the claim, brings reasons and arguments to bear that he hopes will persuade his partner to accept his claim. This is the classic situation studied and reviewed in the Critical Thinking model. A claim C is put forward and reasons 1, 2, and so on are offered for its defense. Further arguments for those reasons may be required, but the bottom line is that one examines the reasons and sees if they properly support the claim. If they do, the Claim C is accepted, if not, it is rejected. Simple, right?

Would that it were so! But just like everything else connected to human beings, it is far more complex, subtle, involved and tortuous than that. First of all, persuasion dialogues vary greatly in the degree of tenacity and attachment to the avowed claim. Secondly, note that I say "avowed claim" because even though a persuasion dialogue is *apparently* about a particular claim, we sometimes change the claim during the course of the argument. This change can happen because our goals become clearer as we discuss matters, or because one partner realizes that the persuasion cannot take place as planned.

Some persuasion dialogues, of course, do not change anyone. An acolyte will never vary from an article of faith, and a politician will never vary from the party line. There is, in these and other cases, no willingness at all to be wrong, to alter, to listen or accept arguments that speak against the claim. Such cases involve what is sometimes called *inauthentic argument*; that is, people who enter into an argument but are not open to change are not putting anything at risk. They might use power, fear or threats, which the early Argumentation Theorist Wayne Brockriede calls "argument as rape," or they might use promises, empty language, and meaningless prose intended to sway without really arguing, which Brockriede called "seduction" (Brockriede 1972).

In order to keep our language consistent and our lexicon modestly sized, I am going to talk about persuasion as having varying degrees along the heuristic/eristic continuum. The key notion to persuasion is still having a fixed claim in mind, and the desire to bring your argument partner over to your point of view. An eristic persuasion dialogue is one where the protagonist, the one who is making the case, has no intention of changing her mind no matter what. These cases include many politicians, most religious arguers, and all teenagers arguing with parents, just to name a few categories. A heuristic persuasion dialogue is one where the protagonist certainly wants to make a case and persuade you, but at the same time allows the possibility of error and, potentially, changes. As opposed to a heuristic inquiry, the protagonist does not go in prepared to change, but the idea is not impossible—change might happen. Most of the arguments we have with friends and family will fall into the category of at least mildly heuristic persuasion. Also in this category are discussions with tradespeople, merchants, and colleagues. But, as you will see in Part 2, you can never be sure what's really at play in an argument.

It is important to pay attention and note how eristic or heuristic a situation you are in. If you are talking to someone who is essentially advocating a position he wants you to take up, and is not indicating it is open for discussion, then different rules apply. The more eristic the situation, the less effort you should put into trying to change someone's mind: it's not going to happen. In these cases it pays just to listen, ask questions, and obtain as much information as possible.

Someone who has a heuristic stance often indicates this by simply listening to what you have to say and answering directly to it. Even those who are not terribly heuristic may in certain circumstances show heuristic elements. A politician out stumping may listen to voters who disagree with him, just because she wants to learn how people see the issues. So, once again, knowing where you are and what kind of argument you are in is essential. In a heuristic persuasion dialogue the most important thing you can do is to listen carefully. What to listen for and how to do it is the subject of the next part, but suffice it to say that most of what you need to know for successful argumentation is being given to you if you know how to listen for it.

So far you have become familiar with three different types of dialogue: heuristic inquiry, negotiation, and persuasion dialogue. Now, of course, I need to point out that these categories are fluid and imprecise. It is not always clear which type you are in, and while knowing is both useful and important, you shouldn't let that bog you down. Moreover, there are frequently shifts from one dialogue to another during a discussion. An argument can begin as a heuristic inquiry, and slide into a persuasion dialogue, then back to a heuristic inquiry. Walton calls this a *dialogue shift*, and lack of awareness of a shift when it happens can result in fallacies and mistakes. If you think, for example, that you are in a heuristic inquiry when in fact you are in a negotiation, then you can fall into a serious error by supposing that your partner is solely interested in the problem at hand and not in just getting a good deal (Walton 1998).

Often a negotiation can slide into a persuasion dialogue when there is some point that one party does not want to budge on, or a persuasion dialogue can become a negotiation when there is room to maneuver. In addition, a heuristic inquiry can move to either a negotiation or a persuasion dialogue and then back when there is some sticking point or obdurate notion that needs special attention. If the shift is dramatic enough, it pays to specifically and clearly move back to the opening stage, state that you feel there has been a change, and ask if you are correct. Imagine that in the Tea for Two example (p. 37) Sophie suggests that maybe some Sundays their staff person could run the store himself. Emma balks and says that they always agreed that one of them would be present when the shop was open, and she is unwilling to change that. Sophie can say something like, "All right, but let me try and persuade you that it wouldn't be awful if we at least tried that." By this statement she announces that they are leaving the heuristic inquiry for a bit to look at this idea, and then they will return.

What if Sophie had simply begun arguing for her point without making that announcement? The risk would be that the context of a heuristic inquiry in which they were operating could be damaged and the entire discussion becomes a persuasion dialogue. The good will and collaboration they were working with could be lost.

By announcing her move, Sophie is bracketing the persuasion dialogue part, and once they are past that they can continue with the heuristic inquiry.

Every bit as important as knowing what kind of argument one is in, is knowing the degree of cooperation: roughly where on the heuristic/eristic continuum does this discussion lie? This will greatly influence the attitude you take, how much trust and honesty you offer, how much credence you give to what is said to you, and how hard you need to look for hidden agendas and unmentioned goals. The more eristic the discussion, the more careful you need to be for the obvious reason that your partner is more concerned with the outcome than the investigation. More of this in Part 2.

1.4 POLEMICS VS. ARGUMENT

It is important to contrast the situations we have been discussing—inquiry, persuasion, and negotiation—to one with a radically different context where you have little or no relation to the audience. For example, you might be making a speech to an audience that is already in agreement with you, and you are exhorting them to a greater level of adherence, or trying to persuade those who are not sure to become sure. A great deal of what you hear these days is not good argument, but what is called polemics: argument designed to make a point aggressively and without being open to disagreement. This often happens in political speeches where the assumption always seems to be that anyone who disagrees with you is absolutely wrong, has nothing interesting to say, and, in fact, is a traitor. The basis of a polemicist's outlook is that no one who disagrees with her is worth listening to. But that's backwards: the fact is, that anyone who believes they can't be wrong is a fanatic, and should be avoided. I first stated this in *How to Win an Argument* (Gilbert 2008), and stand by it now: *No one who believes it is impossible for them to be wrong is worth arguing with.* Of course, it might pay to try, and you might be able to pick up useful information, but if your goal is changing someone's mind, you will be wasting your time.

When an argument is being made to a group or a large audience, the dynamics are very different than when you and I are in a disagreement. When it's one on one, and we know each other, we can question, doubt, probe, and investigate. When I am making a speech to an audience that includes you, there is no possibility of that at all; even more importantly, I'm not interested in hearing you argue with me as it might distract or adversely affect the other listeners. If you are talking to an audience of 500 or 10,000, you cannot care about one individual. Rather, you are concerned with the majority, with imploring them to believe in your position. A polemicist is not interested in disagreement or in open discussion but in straight all out eristic persuasion.

Listening to speeches and reading editorials is something you do frequently, and when you do, your Critical Thinking skills will come in good stead. You should be able to judge the strength of the arguments, the acceptability of the premises and their relevance to the issue. You might even go so far as to imagine a dialogue or consider what the author might say to your objections. This is all very useful, but I feel that your real focus should be with one-on-one or small group arguing. It is in this arena that your opinion is more likely to be affected and where you can have the most impact. It is in the one-on-one where your questions and objections will receive responses. Of course, people are influenced by speeches, and even polemics play a large role in opinion-making, but you should always hold off on full adherence and save your judgment for when you can be involved in questioning and give and take. Speeches are great: if you agree it can confirm your adherence, and if you disagree it can provoke your counter-thoughts, but the focus here is on interactive argumentation where *your* questions and *your* arguments can be addressed and answered. That is where, I believe, you should change your mind if, in the end, you are going to.

Remember that the problem with speeches is that there is little social control, nothing that prevents people from saying anything they can get away with and some things they can't. When you listen you can try and notice if the speaker is dealing with objections and counter-arguments, if consideration is being given to those who disagree. If, to use Johnson's terminology, the "dialectical tier" is being considered (Johnson 2000) Sometimes you may be listening to decent arguments that take opposition into account as, for example, in a Ted talk (a series of talks, often by famous people, sponsored by a foundation, and dedicated to promotion of new ideas, <http://www.tedtalk.com>), but even then you do not have the ability to engage the speaker. The other extreme has been evidenced too often in recent US elections where speechmakers have misrepresented positions, altered history, and straightforwardly lied because they believe they are in the right, and being correct in their views licenses them to do anything in their power to be persuasive. This is much harder to do when in a personal, interactive argument with someone you know, simply because you have the ability to intervene. But even more importantly, people who argue unfairly, who ignore the rules of politeness, communication and reason, suffer social consequences, and people do not want to argue with them.

One final word: paying attention is not always easy. No one pays attention all the time, not me, not you, no one. So mistakes will be made, signals will be missed, and arguments presented will be ignored when they should not be. *If you are not sure where you are, stop and look.* Don't just continue bulling ahead; stop and regroup, ask what's happening, and take the time to marshal your thoughts and re-focus your mind. One of the strongest and most useful argumentative moves you can make is simply to say, "Wait, let me see if I have this right: are you saying ...?"

2

ALL ABOUT ARGUERS

Now that you have an idea of the concept of argument, in this part you will learn about the people you argue with. Mostly we do not argue with strangers, and you will see why that is a vital fact. You will also see that we don't always talk in the same plane and this can be a cause for failure to reach agreement. Looking for agreement is vital, but you also need to be aware of the personality of your argument partners, because these factors always come into play. One such major factor is the gender of the person with whom you are discussing, and you will learn how this is important.

2.1 WHO DO WE ARGUE WITH?

Most of the time we argue with people we know. More importantly, most of the time we argue *with people we will argue with again*. It is unusual, though not unheard of, to have a dispute with someone you don't know and won't encounter again. Generally, your arguments are with friends, family, work and school associates, and neighbors. Not only that, but there is also a plethora of people you see regularly, such as doctors, storekeepers, mechanics, and other people with whom you interact periodically. I call these people your *familiars*, and they play a special role in your life—especially in your argumentative life. We care what all these people think about us, and the closer they are to us the more we care. To most of the world we are our reputations, and whether or not people want to trust us, believe us, interact with us, argue with us, or even just be in contact with us depends on how they view us, how they feel about us, and whether we sound reasonable and reliable. This is called *ethos*.

Mind you, I am not naïve: I know perfectly well that there are people who do not care about anyone's feelings or desires. These people are often considered psychologically damaged and sometimes labeled sociopaths, borderline or psychopaths. There are also people who do not suffer from psychological disorders who are just plain mean, selfish and boorish. These people I label *"super eristic,"* and they live among us. I will say more about the care and feeding of super eristics later, but most of what I have to say depends on your partners' having at least some concern for the mutual relationship you are in.

The fact that we argue mostly with familiars is very significant. First, it means that the opening stage of the argument will either be very quick or non-existent because, since we have had numerous discussions previously, we have already established our working rules. You not only know *who* you are arguing with, but you also know *how* you are going to argue with them. Sure, you might, on occasion, have to return to the opening stage, but you don't have to re-examine the rules you will follow every time you begin; the re-examination will occur when you hit a bump in the discussion. When Athena starts to cry when she's having an argument with Jesse, and he says, "Hey, no fair crying," then they've gone back to the opening stage. Similarly, if Houston tells Caleigh that she won't argue with her if she's shouting, and she says she's not shouting, they have jumped back to the opening stage.

The second most important fact about arguing with familiars is that you share a language. In the largest sense this means that you can understand each other. If someone is presenting me with arguments in Chinese, which I do not speak or understand, then it's a waste of time. Similarly, if there is an abundance of technical terminology being thrown about, then unless you are familiar with it, you can't be involved in the argument. Doctors talking to patients, lawyers to clients, and professors to students or non-experts learn to match their vocabulary to their audience. In fact, we all do this: no one speaks to a toddler the way they do to a peer; we often use different vocabulary for friends, family, colleagues, strangers, and so on. Which brings us to a last important point about language. When we talk with familiars we almost always use short cuts. If I text my friend with the message, Spot at 6? he knows what it means, and he will accept or decline an invitation to meet at our favorite pub, The Auld Spot, at 6 pm without further explanation. Someone else looking at the message out of context would have no idea what it means. She, if invited, would need the full name and address, but even then would likely know I did not mean 6 am.

So one of the important points about familiars is that you share a language. You use the same vocabulary, and you use words, terms and names that have a shared significance. *You understand your shared language.* The less familiar you are with someone, the more careful you have to be in making sure you get their meaning. This is why you feel so different when you are meeting new people or attending a meeting with folks you have not met before. You are on a higher level of alert, more aware of how they are using language, and paying more than usual attention to nuance and subtlety—or, at least, you should be!

The question of language and shortcuts bring us to the essentiality of context. This is a central aspect of the rhetorical nature of communications: words only have meaning in a context. To understand this open any dictionary to a random page or look up a simple word like, 'train,' in *dictionary.com* where you will find more than 20 senses (2012). It is the context, sometimes with the help of grammar, that clarifies which sense is meant. Whether what you travel on, what you do when you teach a dog tricks, what happens to certain sorts of molecules, or what I do when I go to the gym is *disambiguated* by the context, what you know about me, and the subject of our conversation. It is context that filters out the natural ambiguity in language, and when that fails the results can be confusion. Here's a true, funny story.

I am an avid low and slow barbecue smoker and spend a good deal of time in my backyard smoking pork, beef, and chicken and talking about it online. Since our deck is a flight of steep steps above our backyard I have my smoker up on our deck. My wife went to a hardware store once to find some sheets of tin to place under my smoker to protect the deck. She told the clerk that her husband was a smoker, but he always drops ashes on the deck and she was afraid the deck would end up with burn marks. He suggested I give up smoking. She replied, "Oh no, that would be awful, we love his smoking." "You love," asked the perplexed clerk, "his smoking?" My wife insisted she did and that it was great. Eventually he realized that they weren't talking about cigarette smoking, but about making ribs, chicken, and pulled pork. My wife got the tin, and I was back in business smoking my heart out.

Context is everything.

—~~—

Arguments, discussions, dialogues, negotiations, and even quarrels and fights all occur for a variety of reasons. People want to solve a problem, explore an issue, settle a difference, express their feelings, vent their emotions, get what they want, and so on. They all happen for a mix of reasons, but they all have one thing in common: the people involved have goals. Here are some basic facts about goals.

1. Goals are always manifold.
2. Most people are not fully aware of their goals.
3. Goals are often confused with claims.

Let's start with number 1: what does it mean to say that goals are always manifold, or, put another way, how is it that goals are complex? When you get into an argument you know what you want. Emma doesn't want to work on Sundays, and Sophie doesn't want to lose business. But it's never that simple. First of all, Emma doesn't want the business to suffer any more than Sophie does. But also, Emma wants to stay friends with Sophie, wants Sophie to like her, and she does not want to just accede to Sophie's wishes but to understand them as well. Sophie, in her turn, doesn't want Emma to think of her as a workaholic or greedy, but as a caring partner concerned for the welfare of both of them. The point is that there are always other goals—relationship goals or, as they are sometimes called, *face goals*, that come into play. These goals are often at odds with the primary or *strategic goal* that is the original motivation for the dialogue. At the very least they moderate and control them. If I want Mike to give me a lift to the airport and he says he can't, I don't threaten to flatten his tires—it would mean the end of our relationship and certainly the end of lifts to the airport. My face goals are concerned with his opinion of me and his guess at my opinion of him. People who ignore such goals, as we will see in Part 3, end up alone.

You can now see why it is so easy for people not to be aware of their goals, as it states in fact 2. We don't tend to think of face goals in many situations, so we don't take them into account. Mostly they go without saying, and usually it's only when something goes awry that we think of them specifically. Other times, when for example you're asking your boss for a raise, you might be keenly aware of the limits you can go to. While in such situations face goals might be at the forefront of your mind, they are also there, though perhaps to a lesser degree, when dealing with your doctor, auto mechanic, or computer maven. Most of us don't want to alienate people.

The final of the three facts says that goals and claims are often confused. You may think your claim is what you are after, but really there are broader goals you actually want to satisfy. Taken in the logical sense, a claim (or conclusion) is the basis of every argument. "I want a raise," "We should open on Sundays," "Annette should go to sleepaway camp," "We should move our operations to Mexico," are all typical claims. The problem is that when convincing one's partner of the claim is taken to be the only goal, one may miss opportunities to satisfy one's real underlying goals by alternate means. Consider an example we'll call Peter's Camp. Suppose that Kelly and Natalie, Peter's moms, are discussing whether or not Peter should go to sleepaway camp even though he's not very keen. Natalie is against forcing him to do something he doesn't really want to do, while Kelly is afraid that he is not becoming independent enough. She doesn't want him to be a momma's boy, especially since he has two of them.

Kelly has one solution to a problem in mind, but there may be others. If she believes her only goal is to have Peter go to sleepaway camp, then other alternatives that may achieve her more foundational goal of increasing Peter's sense of independence won't be considered. When the *problem* is the focus more than a particular *solution* to the problem, many other options can open up. When you focus on a problem rather than a particular solution, the possibility of increasing the heuristic component of the discussion increases.

One final word: people sometimes have hidden goals, objectives they do not want to bring into the open for any number of reasons. The goal they are hiding might be embarrassing, it might be selfish, or it might involve some objective your partner knows you do not share. Alex might object to a transfer to the downtown store because his ex-girlfriend works there, but he won't admit it. Andrew doesn't want to accept a job as a bartender because he's an alcoholic. Simon doesn't want Alice to go to Gotham Law School because he failed out of there. Whatever the reason, hidden goals can make finding a resolution or changing someone's mind more difficult than it should be. The thing about hidden goals is that you will often have a sense that something is going on that you're not aware of, a feeling that something is not right or confusing. When goals are hidden your argument partner will have difficulty in finding reasons that stand up to inspection because she can't give the reasons she really has. This situation often leads to a lack of clarity, and that can be a clue that there is more going on than you can hear. The truth is, when you feel confused, there's usually a reason: trust your instincts.

2.2 ARGUMENT MODES

Charles Willard pointed out that when people argue they use all the tools available to them, and those tools go well beyond the logical and systematic procedures of both formal and informal logic (Willard 1989). The tools go beyond the words we use, beyond the discursive aspects of our communications. This means, as we discussed above, for example, emotions play an important role in communicating, persuading and demonstrating what is important and what our positions and goals are. In my book *Coalescent Argumentation* I identified four distinct modes of communication. The first mode is the logical mode, and it is characterized by arguments that are linear, have easily identifiable premises and conclusions, and tend to be easily modeled in the Critical Thinking way. Virtually every argument$_1$ and argument$_2$ has at least some logical aspect to it. The second mode is the emotional mode, and we all both send and receive emotional signals that carry important meaning. These signals may partially come from words, but also from tone, context, posture and expression.

The third mode of argument is called the visceral mode, and it includes all aspects of argument that are physical and circumstantial. From a rhetorical point of view a multitude of factors can influence a dispute, and among these many are physical events, settings, or actions. Examples of the role of a setting is when a judge sits behind a high podium and everyone making a case before him is lower, or your boss sits behind a desk while you are in front of it, or he looms over you as he makes his point. But the opposite can also happen: your argument partner might come out from behind a desk to sit beside you, or offer you a beverage, or touch you on your arm, or even just smile. In other words, many actions are communications, and all communications taking place during a dissensual discussion can affect it.

Imagine that during Emma and Sophie's discussion in Tea for Two, that things have slipped off a heuristic inquiry and maybe become just a bit heated. Perhaps Emma has her back up because she is not convinced that Sophie appreciates how important Sundays at home are to her. Now suppose that Sophie, while they are arguing, gets up and makes Emma a cup of tea: the message she is sending is one of caring and concern, and that can ameliorate Emma's sense of security. These actions become part of the *message* that Sophie is sending. Unlike the words you use when you speak, a message is a multi-modal package, a complete communication that sends your intent and your meaning; it uses your body, the context, and any other signal available to make clear what you want to communicate.

The visceral mode of communication is the mode in which all these communicative actions take place. It is the arena in which power roles, gender roles, social roles, as well as actions and events are at play. Sometimes the visceral mode can be the deciding factor in a dispute. If we want to know who is faster, we can race, and the race becomes part of the argument. In this sense sports events can be viewed as arguments over which team or player is best. Similarly, a nod, a smile, an inclination of the head, can all be components in a discussion that may be every bit as important as what has been uttered.

The visceral mode, like all the modes, is not independent of the others. They are interrelated, and while you can use the modes model to describe and help understand, you mustn't expect too much precision from it. For example, one visceral activity very common in your arguments is facial expressions. If your partner smirks during your presentation of an argument that is a visceral component, but you read it as signaling the emotion of disdain. So you must not, as ever, confuse the model with reality.

Not everything we know is physical, and not everything we believe can be empirically tested. Some things like concepts, e.g., friendship and love, are not things that have physical presence, yet we all seem to be able to identify them and understand them. Other things, like ghosts, demons or angels have existences that are highly debated, although a huge percentage of the world believes in some invisible things or others, most notably one or more deities. This makes it obvious that we need to include such references in our argumentation repertoire. If people talk about them and refer to them, then you need to be able to handle them in discussions and argumentative exchanges. All of these ideas ranging from goblins to hunches to concepts fall into the kisceral realm, a term I invented that derives from the Japanese word 'ki' meaning energy.

Arguments in the kisceral realm can be very different because the ways in which kisceral beliefs are confirmed are different. In the kisceral realm you often take things on faith or point to factors that might be considered as irrelevant but are seen as evidence. Very often kisceral arguments require an initial step without which they can't get started. If you do not, for example, accept that a specific sacred text comes directly from God, or that a particular person is a conduit for holy words, then the force of the argument is lost. If we agree on the basic point, (or just accept it for the sake of argument,) then we might well be able to argue about all sorts of ideas, feelings and beliefs that flow from that belief. But in order to get started, there must be some minimum convergence to begin with.

It is worth noting that many of our most basic beliefs, and not just spiritual ones, have a kisceral air about them. Beliefs about the primacy of capitalism or socialism, democracy or fascism, as often as not, have their grounding in matters of faith, for the simple reason that most fundamental credos cannot actually be proven (Sosa 2006). That's why arguments surrounding these matters often bog down: there's no sufficient commonality on which to build any kind of consensus. Even more, there are kisceral arguments that are pretty much everyday. Let me use an example I have used before. Paul looked at a house for sale. He runs into Chris, and they have the following conversation.

"Did you buy that house, Paul?"
"No, Chris, I got a really creepy feeling when I was there, and turned it down."
"But it was such a good price!"
"I don't care if they're giving it away. It gave me the creeps."

We'll call this example The Creepy House, and I think you have to agree that you can understand Paul's thinking. He was in a place that made him feel uncomfortable and would not want to live there. Remember, you do not have to agree that this is a good reason—you just have to understand it. You might even want to argue with him about it and suggest that it's just a bit gloomy and some paint and adding a window would change everything. You do understand: but do remember that understanding and agreeing are not the same thing.

You can see that it can be very important to pay attention to the mode being used. It can help you understand the dynamics of the discussion.

2.3 COALESCENCE

Most of the time we want our arguments to eventually end in agreement. If you are having a heuristic inquiry you want to agree on the results; you want to believe that together you have arrived at the best answer, solution, or belief. In a negotiation you want to agree that the settlement you arrived at is in both your interests and is fair and equitable. In persuasion one partner seeks to have the other agree to their way of seeing things. Arguments that do not end with agreement leave bad feelings and loose ends. You want your familiars to feel good about themselves and feel good about you, and that means being content with the results of the discussion. The best arguments, like the best business deals, always end with everyone feeling like they came out on top. Of course ending an argument may take some considerable time: it may flare up and simmer down, so agreement may be slow in coming (Trapp and Huff 1985).

I have written at length on the idea of Coalescent Argumentation (Gilbert 1997), a style of arguing that is based on agreement, and I still think it is one of the best ways to proceed. The idea is very simple: you try to begin with agreement and work your way forward until you encounter disagreement. Once that happens you can look at where you are and examine how to avoid it. We all agree on many things, but we tend to overly focus on disagreement and allow it to organize and direct a discussion. You need to go back, further and further, into base beliefs and assumptions in order to find the common starting ground. Fisher and Ury wrote, "Behind opposed positions lie shared and compatible interests, as well as conflicting ones" (1981, 43). It is the shared interests that will move you forward, and, frankly, if you really can't find any then you are likely wasting your time trying to reach agreement. Coalescence is the locating of shared values, beliefs and goals so that you can try to merge your interests with those of your partner and build on basic agreements.

A standard, unsophisticated arguer, not at all influenced by Argumentation Theory let alone Coalescent Argumentation, will focus all his thoughts on objections. A fundamental habit many people have is to focus on your reply as soon as *you think* you know what your partner is saying. But if you are working on your reply then obviously, you are not listening to what is being said, but reacting to what you *think is being said.* A level up from that is someone schooled in Critical Thinking: This person listens to the argument and tries to understand its structure and strength, then finds the weaknesses inherent in it. This is better because it entails listening, but can fall short because the listening is superficial and based on locating points of disagreement. There is too much focus on the words and not enough on the message. You can do more.

The Critical Thinking approach is extremely useful, and what you learn there becomes some of the most important tools in your argument toolbox. What I am suggesting is including other tools that go beyond the words being uttered or the words being read. This is not to say that words are not important—they are. But what you have seen so far shows that there is much more going on in a disagreement than what is being said. The emotions of the participants, the multitude and manifold goals, the relationship between the arguers, the kind of dispute in progress, the stage of the dialogue you are in, and so on, all come into play. You must listen not only to the words but also to the myriad meanings, symbols, attitudes, and both apparent and hidden communications being sent to you. You can't just talk to people; you have to read them as well. You need to collect, analyze, and filter their signals in an almost continuous and pretty much instantaneous stream of information. And you do this, mostly, without even thinking about it. What I am suggesting, is that you will do better if you do think about it.

Here's a question I often put to my classes and workshops when I am trying to make the point about how much and how clearly we read people. Consider your current or recent romantic relationship, and if none, then a close family one. How much time does it take for you to know that when you encounter your significant other that something is wrong? Most people say instantly, or, at the most a few seconds. Heck, you can even tell over the phone without seeing them. We are so confident in these judgments that when, for example, Jude says to Olivia, "Is something wrong?" and Olivia replies, "Nothing's wrong," in a short sharp voice, he believes his senses more than her words.

Argumentation Theory, and especially the rhetorical arm of Argumentation Theory, puts a very heavy emphasis on the role of the *audience*. The audience means the person with whom you are arguing, the committee with which you are working, or the community you are addressing. As Chaim Perelman taught us, audience is everything, and an argument must begin with agreement, or, as he put it, a "meeting of minds is indispensable" (Perelman 10). But every audience is different, so in each case you need to find the common ground from which you can begin, an area of shared knowledge among the audience members. This is what Tindale calls a "mutual cognitive environment," which is a shared set of beliefs and/or values of an audience, person or a group (Tindale 1999, 105).

Where do you find this mutual environment in which you both reside? You find it by listening. By listening to your partner you can try and find areas of agreement from which you can begin to locate core disagreement. If that turns out to be impossible, then all you can do is shelve the discussion, walk away from the argument, or halt the negotiations. There is no point in going on. That said, when you are arguing with familiars (which is what we mostly do), if you cannot find agreement you probably haven't tried hard enough.

Finding agreement is a major step in increasing the potential for coalescence, and you should be assiduous in locating it in the correct mode. In other words, emotional agreement (sympathy) or understanding (empathy) is as important as sharing or being sympathetic to beliefs. Please also note that actually believing your partner's precepts is not as essential as understanding them. Either way provides a foundation, but the latter, understanding when you disagree, is more difficult. Still, understanding what it would be like to believe what your partner believes can be very helpful.

The most difficult rule of being coalescent is this: Be more heuristic than your partner. If your dispute partner is being highly heuristic, then you can but match her; however, in most circumstances that will not be the case. Recall that most people are not trained in Argumentation Theory, and their response will often be critical and aggressive. So being more heuristic will not be difficult in most cases. The point is that a heuristic attitude will be met by either a heuristic response *or* an eristic one, but an eristic attitude will always be met by the same, especially from an untrained argument partner. As a result, it makes sense to always be more heuristic than your argument partner.

2.4 ARGUMENTATIVENESS AND AGGRESSIVITY

One of the things you've noticed in your argument adventures over the years is that different people argue in different ways; some seem placid and attentive, while others are quite aggressive and attacking. Not only that, some people seem to like arguing while others tend to avoid it like the plague. These particular characteristics have been identified and examined in social psychology. *Aggressivity* comes in degrees from low to high, with some people being very unaggressive and others being more so. *Argumentativeness* in turn signifies the extent to which a person does or does not like to argue. These two distinct characteristics are central to how an argument will proceed. The degree of argumentativeness, according to Rancer and Avtgis (2006) generally corresponds to more and higher quality arguments, with high argumentatives doing better than low argumentatives. This is not surprising. The more one enjoys argument, the more likely one is to pay attention to it, listen well, and take it seriously.

The factors that enter in here have been investigated by a number of scholars in social psychology, and there is information that can assist you in your argument endeavors. Richmond and

McCroskey (2010, 360), for example, talk about an individual's TFD, "tolerance for disagreement," and how that can impact the way an argument proceeds. Some people quickly become defensive when encountering disagreement, while others are more open. In other words, some people take disagreement as a personal attack, while others see the criticism directed to the argument, and not the arguer. When Caleigh says to Houston, "Did you really think that steak was great?" Houston's hackles immediately go up, and she is prepared to defend herself, whether the disagreement is serious or not. High argumentatives with a corresponding high TFD, will make the best argument partners: they enjoy arguing, but do not take disagreement personally. This is something you can strive for, something you can teach yourself. You can try to focus on the argument as the target for disagreement rather than you yourself. When you enjoy argument and also do not take attacks personally, then you are able to proceed carefully. Of course, the biggest stumbling block to this is itself the very reason we argue: disagreement.

Most of us, most of the time, do not find disagreement unpalatable. Yet, as you saw above, many factors can come into play that color the disagreement and influence the way the discussion may go. The awareness of goals, the degree to which you see them as in conflict, the level of attachment to them, and the amount of personal involvement all enter into forming the quality of the argument. Remembering that we almost always argue with familiars, we frequently know what to expect; you have an awareness of your partner's degree of argumentativeness and tolerance for disagreement. It pays for you to take these matters into account when preparing for an argument.

The aspect of argument that most of us dislike is aggression. No one likes to feel attacked or under siege. You have surely known a manager who relies on aggression backed up by authority to achieve agreement, and such people are both disliked and rarely successful in the long run. Compliance is not persuasion. We know that someone who is high in aggressivity "will have their arguments judged poorly" (Infante, Rancer, and Jordan 1996), and even rejected because of their demeanor. The opposite of aggressivity is agreeableness, and not surprisingly it has the opposite results. When someone is agreeable and appears to be interested and listening, their arguments are judged more favorably.

Consider an example we'll call The Audit. A large organization with over 5,000 employees and a large plant needs to have a washroom audit. This is due to legislation requiring accessible washrooms for the handicapped as well as a desire for gender neutral bathrooms to accommodate transgender employees. The audit involves inspecting each and every washroom and listing its facilities and accessibility. At a meeting to discuss this, the Vice President of facilities (VP) meets with his plant manager (PM). Imagine the difference in these two brief conversations.

> The Audit [A] VP: "We need to get this job done right away," he says to PM. She nods agreement, and says, "I understand, but it's a huge job." VP responds with, "I told the president not to worry about it, so I don't care how huge it is! Just get it done. Top priority."

> The Audit [B] This time when PM responds, VP says, "Well, I told the president not to worry about. I know it is a big job and it has to be done right. What resources do you need? Can we work out a time line?"

In [A], the immediate response demonstrates high aggressivity, and you can imagine that PM will not feel good about it. In fact, she will likely react with stress, and may come back with an aggressive retort, like, "Well, if you gave me the people I need, then maybe things would get done!" In [B] that response would not be appropriate, because the stress is being shared. The acknowledgment that the job is a big one and might need additional resources indicates an agreeableness and an understanding.

How people react in arguments is a result of a number of factors, primarily culture and socialization. Your parents raised you in a particular culture, but they often also gave you your attitude to argument. Whether or not you become defensive about arguing, take conflict personally, approach or avoid arguments, are more often than not the result of your upbringing (Hample and Cionea 2010). I, for example, was raised in Brooklyn, NY, where *not* to argue was considered insulting: it meant you weren't listening and not taking your partner seriously. If you didn't argue it meant you weren't willing to go to that much bother, because you didn't think what was said was important enough. On the other hand, there are cultures where arguing is considered rude and one does not do it, especially in straightforward ways. Being aware of this will become important later on when we talk about discovering the rules of argument. It's also important to think in cultural terms as we turn to the next section and consider the role of gender in argument.

2.5 GENDER AND ARGUMENT

First of all, we have to be clear *and careful* about how we generalize when we talk about gender. While on the one hand we may seem to recognize differences between the way in which *many or most* women and men as groups argue, there are any number of other factors that can enter in and even override gender. These factors include culture, geography, age, education and personal background. In other words, there may be generalizations about women and men that more or less work across the board, but it still means that a woman from New York City might have an argument style closer to a man from New York City than she does to a woman from Winnipeg. Not only that, but some research indicates that level of education is one of the most important factors in similarity/dissimilarity of communicating. More partners who are both college educated will argue like each other than partners who have different levels of education. So, to begin with, gender is one of a number of factors to be taken into account rather than the only one or even the major one.

In our culture there are widely held beliefs about the differences between women and men. The belief that women experience more emotions than men do is a very common one. However, research shows this is not the case. Rather, women and men generally *experience* the same amount of emotion, but women *express* more emotion. The social roles assigned to each gender dictate how you express what you feel. Women expect themselves to react more negatively to sad things, and men less so (Rancer and Avtgis 2006). The emotion men are most comfortable expressing is anger, as it is a signal of dominance. However, women do show more anger than men in domestic argumentation, but it is not even clear that men are more aggressive than women in many other situations (Frodi, Macaulay and Thome 1977). *It is the role you are expected to play* that is the major factor in your expression. Some young men are aware of this and have the insight to view it as a limiting factor and a burden (Edwards and Jones 2009), but that does not make it go away.

We expect women to be more emotional and caring, to avoid conflict more than men, and to use less aggression than men. Pairs of women and men reading identical scripts that illustrate conflict and aggression have been judged differently by observers depending on the sex of the pair (Infante, Rancer, and Jordan 1996). A pair of women reading an identical script as a pair of men are judged as being more aggressive than the men. For this reason, among others, women may avoid *seeming* aggressive, even when they are *feeling* aggression. This has consequences for arguing: For men being argumentative is considered a positive trait—a sign of authority or leadership, but when women argue they are more often labeled as aggressive rather than argumentative, and aggression is a negative quality. It is, if you will, a double-bind: It's good to be argumentative, considered a quality important for success, yet when women demonstrate that quality they are often judged as aggressive, which is not correlated with success.

The differences in the way in which many women and many men communicate have led to serious relationship problems and inequities. However, this book is not primarily about how people *should* argue, but how they *do* argue, which means you want to know about the argumentation culture as it actually is. In our culture as reported by Deborah Tannen (1990), men and women communicate in different ways. It is important to be aware that it is more accurate to talk about feminine and masculine styles, rather than woman and man styles, because many factors can influence your style. Male teachers, social workers, stay at home dads, and others who are in positions where they have to listen carefully to feelings, mood and attitude often have skills associated with women. Similarly, women often "code switch," to use Lakoff's term (1990), which means they use one form of communication when at work and another when talking with other women or family.

This is not the place for an extended discussion of woman/man communication differences, as that is a book in itself. (Deborah Tannen's *You Just Don't Understand: Women and Men in Conversation*, is still in print, and still interesting and fun.) The easiest way to think about the differences is one that describes the differences between woman-speak and man-speak as similar to that of two distinct cultures (Maltz and Borker 1982). Just as you would be sensitive to how someone from another country is speaking to you, so you should do the same with someone of another gender. Women tend to avoid conflict more than men do, just as some Asian cultures avoid conflict more than western, and showing emotion is acceptable in some cultures, but not others.

The plaint often made about cross-gender arguments is that you don't know what rules to follow. Lisa tells Paul about a problem at work, and he responds with a suggestion of how to fix it, but Lisa reacts negatively. What did he do wrong? Simple: he followed the wrong rule. He followed the masculine "respond to a problem with a solution" rule, rather than the feminine, "respond to a problem with sympathy" rule. In Lisa's culture, feminine culture, the first reaction is empathy, a demonstration of understanding. In Paul's culture the reaction is not sympathy, but solution: here's how to fix it. It is worth noting that the male response demonstrates superiority over his partner, while the female mode demonstrates equality with hers. These are cultural differences (Lakoff 1990).

So how do you learn the rules? How do you know how to play the game in a supportive and shared way? Glad you asked, because that's the topic of Part 3.

3

ARGUING WITH PEOPLE

In Part 1 you learned about arguments and in 2 about arguers. In this part you will put those together to see how best to proceed in an argument. You will see that there are rules, and those rules flow from the inter-personal dynamics of the actual social situation. You will see that knowing about arguments and arguers leads to an awareness that can foster agreement and good argument.

What is a good argument?

There are good arguments, bad arguments, inconclusive arguments, suspended arguments, constructive arguments, silly arguments, weak arguments, and powerful arguments; a myriad of other adjectives can be applied as well. Mostly, though it comes down to the same thing: just what is a good argument? While the answer to that question is not simple, it's a very good idea to look at it closely.

First of all, going back to a distinction made in Part 1, are we thinking about an argument$_1$ or an argument$_2$? Some of the adjectives apply to one, some to the other, and some to both. A silly argument, for example, can be an argument$_1$ or an argument$_2$: "If John buys a lottery ticket, then he'll certainly win the $25 million." That argument$_1$ is silly because lotteries don't work that way. On the other hand, we might have a lengthy argument about something very trivial, say, about where we would live if we won that lottery, and realize we were just being foolish. It gets worse. Depending on how we value the arguments we're discussing, they might be good in some ways and bad in others. The trivial argument might have been conducted very well with consideration, attentiveness, and all those nice things, even though the whole topic was silly.

Second is the question of what kind of dialogue we are in. A good argument in a heuristic inquiry might not be a good one in a persuasive inquiry. Negotiating is something else entirely; in negotiation you want to give away as little as possible, while in a heuristic inquiry that's simply not an issue. In this part of the book you are going to understand the place of rules in argumentation, as well as how to determine what they are. To begin with you need to become yet more familiar with three terms that have come up before. They are, perhaps the three terms most central to this whole enterprise:

3.1 HEURISTIC, ETHOS, AUDIENCE

One of the key ways that arguments differ is in the degree of cooperation between the participants. Typically, arguments range from the heuristic inquiry, which has the highest degree of cooperation, through negotiation, where we each want the greatest benefits but also want both parties to feel satisfied, and on to persuasion, where you know what you believe and try to bring your partner around to that belief. The problem is that you have to figure out how heuristic (or eristic) your partner is, and that is not always easy. You know there are people who never believe they're wrong; and even if caught with no retreat they find a way out. They are inherently eristic and feel that their ego is tied into winning and being right; such people tend to be high in aggressiveness. Others are not wholly eristic but have areas or subjects in which they are unyielding. It is possible, of course that there are people who are always heuristic, but such a Buddha-like argumentative state, if it exists, is rare indeed.

The truth is that the factors that go into how heuristic an argument will be are manifold. The topic of discussion, the personal history you have with your partner, what is (or what is thought to be) at stake, the present mood of the disputants, the power and gender relations, the setting, and even the weather can or will come into play. If this sounds farfetched, if you don't imagine all these things may be relevant, consider how you assess the context and timing when you are planning to bring up a controversial matter. If you expect disagreement from your argument partner, be it your business associate or spouse, you will, when possible, ask yourself, "Is this a good time?" In doing that, you are taking the context, including the mood of your partner, into account. If my manager has just returned from a meeting with her manager and seems harried and then looks up at me with a, "What now?" expression, I will forgo my request to change my vacation slot until another time. This is only sensible.

People tend to be heuristic when they do not feel threatened. If you feel someone wants something from you and you are not sure what it is or why they want it, you will tend to be more guarded, cautious, and less willing to agree. When things are out on the table, *and you feel that your partner is open to change*, then you will be more ready to listen. This means that you need to have an understanding of both your partner and yourself, and that, in turn, means having a real appreciation of your goals, objectives, and beliefs and those of your partner. In the Tea for Two example, (p. 37) Sophie is aware and appreciative of Emma's need not to work on Sundays, and this means that Emma can listen to Sophie's ideas without fear of having her own goals ignored or trampled. Notice that Emma is clear about her goal; she knows that her goal is *not* to keep the shop closed on Sunday but rather that she not work on Sunday. Even this small degree of sophistication allows for a more heuristic interaction.

Going from the simple case of Tea for Two to something much more complex still leads to the same considerations. Major union negotiations, for example, must keep in mind that the union negotiators must *appear* in a certain way to their members. More than once a union leadership has been bounced out of office because negotiations went too smoothly for too many years—a very unfortunate but real attitude. As incredible as it sounds, the emotional needs of the membership to appear strong can have an overriding influence on the future. So the apparent goal of a negotiation might be a good contract, but the negotiators have other goals as well, and they must also be considered. For this reason the more people involved in a disagreement the more complex it is likely to become, as the number of goals and objectives increases many times over.

As indicated above the focus of *Arguing with People* is primarily one-on-one or small group discussion. The dynamics of speeches, of addressing large audiences, is very different from the dialogue that occurs with familiars. As mentioned earlier, a politician making a speech is a completely different story from an employee trying to persuade a manager to increase break time, and two politicians having a so-called debate is nothing like a couple deciding to buy a house. One main reason for this is our second key idea, *ethos*.

Ethos corresponds loosely to someone's reputation or character, but as we use it the word has more of a focus on the ideas of honesty, reliability and personal history. Each of your familiars has a certain ethos in your eyes, and that has been built up over time. You know people you "trust with your life," and others you "wouldn't trust as far as you could throw them." You have friends who are always late and others who are invariably on time; you have co-workers who never fail to complete tasks and others who need prodding. All of these are components of ethos, and it controls how you deal with someone and how they deal with you.

When you first meet someone you tend to accept them in a more or less positive way; most of us are fairly trusting, but within limits. If you are too trusting, you are considered gullible, and if you are not trusting at all, you are considered cynical. Most of us are in between, and we tend to look favorably on people *until they abuse that favor*. The new worker who tattles, the boyfriend who cheats, the partner who is disrespectful, or the associate who doesn't carry her weight, all begin to slip in your estimation, thereby lowering their ethotic status. By the same token, the co-worker who covers for you, or the friend who understands that you did not mean to be late, raises their ethotic standing.

Ethos is a complex phenomenon in part because someone can have a high standing in one category but not in another. Someone whose work you respect might not be someone in whom you are comfortable confiding. It's also easy for someone to drop dramatically in your ethotic evaluation. Someone who disappoints you in some serious way may have to work hard over a long time to restore his standing. This standing is important because it determines how open you feel you can be with someone when arguing. If you are having a disagreement and you feel you are talking with someone you can trust, someone who shares your interests and is focused on problem solving rather than winning, then you can proceed more openly and less tactically than with someone you don't feel so positive about.

How we evaluate ethos depends a great deal on the context, our goals, where we are arguing, and what we are arguing about. All of this can be wrapped into the term *audience*. Whenever you speak with someone you adopt a particular approach based on who you believe they are and what you imagine their goals to be. If you encounter someone who sounds like a foreigner and has a bewildered look, you will assume your "help the tourist" mantle: you'll put on a smile and try to look unthreatening and helpful. If your manager is talking to you, you will look interested and keen so as to portray your usefulness to him.

A very important aspect of audience is to understand what beliefs you share, what you have in common. Many scholars, notably Perelman, Brockriede, Hample, Willard, and Tindale, among others, emphasize that without some shared values and beliefs, argument cannot proceed. This means that if we don't have at least some minimum values and outlooks in common, we have no basis on which we can get started. Moreover, when arguing what you really want to do is begin with shared beliefs, and build from them to the contentious point—*you always want to begin with agreement.* In Tea for Two, Sophie and Emma agree that they do not want to harm the business but also agree that Emma needs time with her family. This shared starting point, accepted *and respected* by both, means that they can explore further options together. When a union and management are negotiating and they both agree that the economy is in trouble and that the business is suffering, they can work from that starting point. In a persuasion dialogue, finding common ground is also essential: you need to find that common ground in order to begin building your agreement from that point.

There are very few people with whom you do not have something in common, and certainly none among your familiars. In fact, there is often a great deal that is taken for granted and need not be discussed in detail or at all. These beliefs and values enable you to communicate without re-establishing the essential commonality necessary to argue. If this isn't the case, then it is necessary to stay at the opening stage until a sufficient commonality is established. When Jude and Olivia are negotiating, and Jude says, "We do want the business to keep going, right?" Jude is emphasizing a common belief that while initially taken for granted may have come into doubt. Beyond such audience specific beliefs lay a set of values most of us take for granted: pleasure is better than pain; education is good; family obligations are paramount; life is better than death. Such beliefs are called *loci* by Perelman, and do not normally come into dispute (though note, like everything else, they might).

Let me be especially philosophical for a moment. You know that when you want to defend a claim, you provide a reason. You want to lower tuition costs, and your reason is that an educated populace is good for democracy. Now that reason itself can be questioned and, in turn, becomes a claim that needs a reason. Why is an educated populace good for democracy? Well, you explain, educated people are less likely to be duped by despots or charismatic dictators because they require reasons for beliefs. If your partner then asks, "What's so wrong with dictators?" you are headed for an infinite regress. This means that every reason you announce will be itself questioned and another reason demanded. While this is a favorite game of philosophy majors (and three year olds), it rarely happens in real life, and the reason for this is the presence of loci, commonly held beliefs. As we go further and further back in our reasons, we normally reach some place where questioning the reason is simply silly. So philosophy majors notwithstanding (because it is after all their job), if we get into an infinite regress it means we do not have sufficient commonality to pursue the discussion.

3.2 WATCHING THE PROCESS

We have all had the experience of our attention wandering. You know what I mean: you're reading a book and suddenly realize you didn't absorb a word for the last two pages (happens to students all the time), or you are watching a TV show and become aware that you were not paying attention at all. The fact is you can only pay attention to so much at once. If you are focused on one thing, then the others will slip by you, which is why paying attention to your dispute partner is so vitally important. I'm in the habit, for example, of listening to an audio book while walking my dog, and I know that even something as simple as crossing the street can divert my attention from the plot.

When arguing, regardless of the type of dialogue, you must pay attention to two things. The first is what is being said to you, and the second is the person who is saying it, and both of these are equally important. First of all, words by themselves have no meaning; they must be understood in a context. Imagine that you are giving a presentation at work, and when you wake up that morning you see that the streets are completely blocked by a blizzard, and there is no way you can possibly get to work. You say, "Great."

Now how do I, who happen to be eavesdropping, know what you mean? You could mean, Great: I have more time to prep my presentation; or, you could mean Great: I'm all primed and ready to go and now I have to delay and stew for another day. Only *your* tone of voice, and *my* knowledge of *you* can help me fill in that information.

So you have to pay attention to what is being said, how it is being said, and who is saying it. In other words, you have to listen to the message, and not just the words. That's a lot, especially when the tendency to think about what you are going to say rather than listen to what is being said is so strong. But the fact is, a great deal of what you need to know is being given to you by your partner, and without that information you cannot know how to proceed. Put simply, if you do not understand what your argument partner's goals, objectives, beliefs and feelings are, you really have no idea whether to even agree or disagree, let alone how to do it. Going back to Tea for Two (p. 37), if Sophie only knows that Emma does not want to open on Sundays and misses her reason why, then in all likelihood she will be arguing at cross purposes. The problem for Emma may *appear to be* not opening on Sundays, but when Sophie listens, she understands that Emma's most important goal is being with her family and not that the shop stay closed.

The problem is, in one sense, that people often don't really know what they want, and if you want to argue successfully, then you have to figure it out. It may sound strange to you when I say that most people don't know what they want, but please throw your mind back to our discussion about goals. We tend to focus on one goal that is often a solution to a problem that we ourselves thought of, and this locks out other possibilities that may both solve the problem, satisfy our goals, and do so in a way that also satisfies our partner's goals. Two minds really do work better than one, because the way you see the solution to a problem may very well be better than the way I see it.

The other aspect of the communication relationship existing between you and your partner is the importance of maintaining a careful awareness of affect, an awareness of the emotions and feelings being expressed. If a dispute partner is expressing anger, frustration, or becoming short-tempered, then you need to assess what is going on. Discomfort on the part of an inquiry partner can be indicative of many things, and it is vital to pay attention and try to figure out its cause. Often there is some hidden goal or agenda, and the discussion is coming too close to it. Other times the outcome is more important to your partner than you realized.

The biggest clue available to you is your own sense that "something's going wrong." We are all animals, and like most animals we have instincts and senses that warn us of many things. From infancy on we learned to pay attention to the feelings of our parents and caretakers, becoming aware when we were pushing too hard or when their mood began to change. Our lives, after all, depended on it. As we got older we became attuned to our friends and colleagues, sensing their pleasure and displeasure and reacting to it. Failure to have this capacity is considered a mental health disorder, because understanding the feelings of other people is a natural component of surviving. When you sense that there is something going on with your partner, you're probably right: your instincts are usually correct.

To be a good arguer you need to be in tune with the people you are interacting with. Imagine Laird and his wife Shazia returning home from a dinner party hosted by Jude and Olivia. Laird says, "I can't understand how Olivia could be that upset, just because Jude forgot to take the ice cream out of the freezer." Shazia looks over at Laird, raises her eyebrows, and says, "Her upset had nothing to do with the ice cream." Laird blinks and says, "It didn't?" In order to argue well, you have to be attuned like Shazia, and not take things at their surface level like Laird.

While it's true that some people come to emotional sensitivity naturally, many others learn it through their occupation, role in life, or interest in other people. Women, teachers, social workers and others in the helping professions all need to be aware of the emotional issues in front of them. Women learn from an early age that they need to read children as well as the frequently more powerful and stronger men surrounding them. Others in the helping professions, taken in a broad sense, learn to read those they are teaching and helping—assuming they are good at their jobs. Of course there are exceptions, but the generalities make the point.

Recall earlier when I asked how long it takes you on arriving home to know that something is wrong with your spouse, partner, boyfriend or girlfriend? Unless you are really not paying attention the awareness can be instant—even on the phone! That's how attuned we are to our familiars. You are also attuned to those with whom you interact less often, though perhaps not so highly. Still, when the young woman who always makes your morning coffee at the local coffee shop is upset, you are very likely to notice. When the meeting with your manager or professor does not go well, you should be able to reflect on it and see if you missed something or made a wrong move given the emotional atmosphere. The important point is that by listening and paying attention to the *message* which contains both the information being sent to you and the affective and emotive components, you can argue and communicate in a rich and rewarding way.

3.3 THE MOST IMPORTANT BELIEF YOU CAN HAVE

One of the points you saw in the last section was that people are often unaware of many aspects and variations in their goals. This does not only apply to your partners, but to ourselves as well. You might think you know what you want, but someone else might have a better way or a more congenial and cooperative way of getting you there. One of the reasons for this unawareness is that we all tend to be very fixed in our beliefs. Changing our minds is not something we do easily or lightly. Of course, there are beliefs that we hold far more strongly than others, and lightly held beliefs are much easier to change. If I think, for example, that my friend and I are going to a baseball game a week Wednesday and he sends me a message saying we can meet before the game on Thursday, I'll check it out, and if I have to I'll alter my thinking. On the other hand, if I were somehow convinced that I am mistaken that I live in Toronto, I would almost certainly believe I was having a nervous breakdown.

Think of it this way: our beliefs form a web—they are all connected, and as we get to the center of the web, our beliefs are more and more connected, and, therefore, more and more difficult to change. It's like the game of pick up sticks: you just can't take one from the middle without upsetting the others; you have to work carefully from the outside in. Changing someone's mind is like that, and unless you pay attention to their web of beliefs, you will have difficulty making progress. People hold onto their values and beliefs for a reason: weakness in the web is discomfiting; it creates insecurity and uncertainty, states we prefer to avoid. We resist being wrong, changing our minds, and admitting to error, but, I want to urge, this is just a habit and one that is deleterious to good communication and argumentation. Rather than clinging to our beliefs and values, we should always be prepared to change, improve and alter them.

I have a mantra that I teach to my students and impart to my workshop participants:

REMEMBER: No matter what—you may be wrong!

The ancient philosophers who held this belief were called skeptics, and they felt there was no absolute truth, and nothing that couldn't be falsified. This was later relied upon by Sir Karl Popper (1979), who argued that while we can know we are wrong, we can never be certain we are right. Everyone knows there is no such thing in nature as a black rose, but no matter how many red and white and pink roses we see, our claim will become false if a single black rose is discovered in some faraway jungle.

Everything can be false. Take one of the most simple and basic truths: 1 + 1 = 2. Obviously, if anything is true this is. But now think about what happens if you add two colors together: you don't get two colors, you get one. So, in this case, 1 + 1 does not equal 2. Speaking broadly, you argue about one of two things, facts or values. When there is a disagreement about facts there is no point in arguing—we just look it up. When that does not work, it means that we disagree about the sources of evidence we are using. Remember the Triple Play example (p. 31): if I, a diehard Blue

Jays fan, insist there was a triple play, then I am relying on what I saw rather than the record book. You may insist that the Baseball Almanac is the appropriate authority, but when I disagree, we end up arguing about how we decide the claim. The word 'honor' is spelled just like that in the US, but in British countries is spelled 'honour.' Which is correct depends on what authorities we choose to use.

This is important because it affects the way in which you need to view your positions and those of your partner. If you go into a situation believing that you have the truth and can't be wrong, your ability to listen will be greatly diminished. But if you are open, and can include aspects of your dispute partner's position into yours, then you can make much more progress. In a negotiation, respecting why your partner desires certain goals, can help move it along. Even in a heuristic inquiry trying to see the world the way your partner sees it, and understand why she is making the points she is, can help get to the best answer.

One final philosophical point regarding my mantra "believe nothing." You probably want to point out to me that the statement: *No matter what—you may be wrong!* could itself be wrong, and this results in a paradox. Yes, that's correct, and it's correct because the world is paradoxical. It's *we* who make sense of the world, not the world that explains itself to us. 'Nuff said.

3.4 THE RULES

Everyone knows that many times there is a difference between what we *do* as opposed to what we *ought to do*. You ought to come to a full stop at each and every stop sign, but we almost always roll just a bit. You ought to begin work on that essay or project well before the due date, but, well, that doesn't always happen, does it? It's against the rules to keep a book out of the library beyond the due date, but many people do it. What we ought to do is governed by norms and rules that are not always followed, or, if they are then not followed religiously. Arguing is no different.

Soon, I am going to describe two different sets of rules that are useful in an important way. But first, just one example to emphasize the way rules are sometimes loosely followed. One rule usually propounded in Critical Thinking courses is that you ought not put forward any statement as a reason that you cannot prove, with a milder version saying you ought not put forward a statement you do not have a reason to believe. But nonetheless, depending on the context, the audience and other factors, it might make sense to do just that. You might, for example, in a negotiation make it seem like something you are giving up is more important to you than it really is. Or, in a persuasion dialogue, you might pretend to adopt a value held by your partner in order to make a point. We do this with children continually as when we all ooh and ah over a plate of chicken fingers laid before them in a restaurant. So sometimes when we have a rule we are supposed to follow, we actually don't much of the time. Nonetheless, rules do apply and they are something we all rely on, and this will be expanded upon in what follows.

I will use the terms 'rules' and 'norms' interchangeably They are things we make up and enforce with punishments or by cultural and social reactions and consequences. In law there are many rules regarding how to argue in court and even in business negotiations. For example, in most jurisdictions it is illegal in a negotiation to withhold pertinent information such as a leaky basement or impending lawsuit. But most arguments are not governed by strict rules: You will generally not be arrested for raising your voice, but you might alienate your argument partner. This is one of the reasons I keep stressing the idea of familiars.

—␣␣—

The ideal rules of argument have long been sought after and debated. Since the times of Ancient Greece philosophers have been the custodians of argument and reasoning. Philosophers have studied argumentation, created systems, both of formal and informal logic, the first being much more rigid and technical than the latter. The very idea of fallacies, common mistakes in reasoning, was an invention of philosophers, specifically to aid in the teaching and improvement of arguing, discussing and problem solving.

While there have been many systems and thousands of textbooks produced in the Critical Thinking industry, there are just a few basic ideas that I want to very briefly remind you about. Critical Thinking is closely connected to the area of Informal Logic which focuses primarily on arguments and their internal relations. The emphasis is on the ways in which reasons, also known as premises, relate to and support claims, also known as conclusions. One popular model first introduced by Ralph Johnson and Tony Blair in 1977, and reproduced in a myriad of variations, lists three aspects, Relevance, Sufficiency and Acceptability: The reasons for a claim must be relevant, they must be strong enough, and they must be seen as "true enough" or acceptable to the audience. In addition, the premises must hang together well enough to be adequate to form a reliable argument. As all of this, and much more is covered in the standard Critical Thinking course which you are taking or have taken, I am not going into details, but you might want to look at your own textbook and see how these ideas are played out. However, there is an important point to be made.

You might think after completing your required course in Critical Reasoning, or taking that one or two day workshop in Critical Thinking, that the rules are sort of irrelevant. Who, after all, is going to analyze an argument, scan it out, make a pretty diagram of how the premises relate to the conclusion? Who is going to inspect each reason for relevance, for fallacies? Who will follow closely enough to decide on the adequacy of the logic being used? The answer is, you. You do it all the time, and you do it better when you have taken that Critical Thinking course and performed those exercises and analyzed those letters to the editor.

Whenever someone presents you with an argument, a reason for a claim, you might say, "You can't say that!" or, "What? That doesn't make sense!" or, "That doesn't follow at all." Whenever that happens you are using your Critical Thinking skills. You may not be able to pinpoint the problem like an Argumentation Theorist or Critical Thinking instructor, but your senses have been tuned. It's like when you learn a new word and suddenly hear it popping up in conversation regularly. Or, when you learn the meaning of 'penultimate' is not, "the very ultimate," but "next to last," and suddenly you notice when people use it incorrectly. This happens with fallacies as well. Hample (2007) points out that research shows that only one fallacy (argument based on pity) is accepted more than 20% of the time, and most far less frequently than that. This means that the information you have about argumentation creates triggers in your mind that help you notice both bad and good arguments. So every time you think, "Hey, that doesn't follow," you can thank your Critical Thinking instructor.

Another aspect of the rules that are often taught has to do with fairness. While Critical Thinking does not focus on this idea all that much, courses in English, Communications, and Rhetoric do emphasize this aspect. The Amsterdam School of Pragma-dialectics, to mention one leading group in Argumentation Theory, places a great deal of emphasis on discussion participants being able to make and defend arguments and respond to objections. The rules in this approach, while not using the term 'fairness,' emphasize freedom to critique and defend without being limited, including by non-verbal means. The philosopher Jürgen Habermas (1990) also felt strongly that good argument could only take place in a context of freedom and openness where power and privilege were equalized. In these approaches, the signal expression might be, "That's not fair!"

The ideal is when we all have a level playing field, but what about the real? Here are three very important points to remember. First, human beings are social animals; secondly, arguing, in any way, shape or form, is a social activity; thirdly, all social activity is governed by rules. As a result of this, argument, like all social activity, always has rules governing behavior. Argument rules are not really written down the way driving rules are but are rather informal and social the way queuing up or behaving in a restaurant is. In some cultures, to use queuing or lining up as an example, the activity is socially regimented. There are rules against breaking into a line, jumping to the head, holding someone's place, and so on. Some cultures have even more complex and subtle rules, and yet others take pushing and shoving for granted.

If you think of social rules, you can notice how distinct they are and how precise. In North America the audience at an opera or concert sits extremely silent, trying to not even cough. In Italy, by comparison, if the audience is not pleased with the performance they will be very vocal about it. At the same time, at a rock concert in the US, noise is expected, and if you want to listen carefully to the music, you'd best get the CD or download. At a sports event you can shout at the top of your lungs, but certainly not at a symphony. The context and situation are always what determine the rules, and we can get into embarrassing situations if we confuse them or don't know them.

The rules governing argumentation are no different, and there are two main intertwined aspects that govern them: context and audience. Context covers a wide range of aspects that are crucial and fall under the mode I have referred to above as visceral. The broadest sense of context refers to culture, such as whether you are in New York, Houston, Tokyo, Dubai, or Toronto. Each location has been influenced by geographical, historical, social, and cultural traditions that dictate how disagreement is going to proceed. In some places disagreement is strongly downplayed, while in others it is savored and enjoyed. But for your purposes context typically refers to a much narrower realm than culture and geography. For your purposes the issue is more of whether you are at work, with friends, at home, or in a classroom or workshop; this local context forms an important part of being aware of the rules. The rules are formed from a matrix that is a blend of where you are, who the participants are, and what personal and power relationships are in play.

All of the ideal rules, whether Informal Logic, Pragma-dialectics, or Habermas's, assume or desire a level playing field. In argumentative terms this would be one where non-logical considerations such as power, ability, resources, personal background and status played no role at all. I am not about to say that this never happens, but I will say it is the exception and not the rule. This is for the simple reason that *there are always relationship goals at play in every social interaction*. Remember, that most of the time we are arguing with familiars, and that means we know them, have a relationship with them, *and care about that relationship*. While this is always the case with familiars, it is also the case with many other people we encounter. In business, even when you are not going to meet someone again, your reputation and that of your company are important, so you want to be well thought of. Your after-school job may involve dealing with a lot of strangers, but you want your manager to think well of you and provide a letter of reference or a promotion.

So there are always rules, *but we don't always know what they are*. In familiar situations there will likely be few surprises. When Larry and Jorge are arguing about sports at the pub after work, they both know how hard they can push, the kind of language they can use, what rules to follow, the values at play, and just how seriously to take the issue on the table. Similarly, when Rosa and Andrea are sharing intimacies they too know the rules by which they are communicating. The proof of this is when something goes wrong. If Jorge suddenly becomes cross at Larry's remark about the Boston Red Sox, Larry is liable to say something like, "Hey, man, chill—what's going on?" By the same token if Andrea seems cold to Rosa, Rosa may also ask what's going on: Did she do something? Is something wrong?

In other words, when the rules do not appear to be working, we stop and assess: was a rule broken? Was there a violation of a protocol that went unnoticed? Or, as may well happen, has the subject changed? Maybe Jorge is really upset about something that happened at work, and it's leaking into your sports chat. In these situations we need to return to the opening stage or even the confrontation stage. The opening stage, you will recall, is where the rules are established, or, as often as not, taken for granted. If they've changed, we need to examine them more closely than we did before. It may also be that we are not arguing about what we thought we were arguing about. Larry thought he and Jorge were arguing about baseball and he could tease and taunt Jorge as usual. In fact, Jorge was reacting to a humiliation he suffered at work, and they need to return to the confrontation stage to reassess the topic of their discussion.

Rules are funny things, because even though they exist they are not always followed. We don't always come to a full stop at a stop sign, and we don't always travel at exactly the speed limit. The majority of people will go 5 to 10 miles or kilometers above the limit, because while it is not the rule it is the norm. Norms are customs that are followed in different contexts, and they may or may not mirror the rules. Speed limits are a perfect example. In some places a driver adhering strictly to the limit may receive dirty looks and mutters from other drivers. On the other hand, when we are some place where we know the police patrol a lot, we keep strictly to the limit and call it a speed trap. On yet another hand, someone whizzing by at an outrageous speed will also get condemning looks from other drivers because he is violating the norm, even though most of us giving the looks are also speeding.

The same is true when it comes to argument. We do not expect each other to argue in some mechanical, rigid way. An arguer will use word choice, tone of voice, body position and a host of other tactics both conscious and unconscious to further her position while at the same time not going so far as to commit egregious errors.

Going too far is like the speeding driver going 50 miles an hour over the limit and weaving in and out of lanes. You don't want to be near that person and may feel pleased if you see them getting a speeding ticket, even if you yourself are exceeding the limit by 10 miles or so. They are breaking the rules and violating norms in an unacceptable way and should suffer the consequences. The drivers you like having around you are those with a similar outlook on driving safety, habits and courtesy. There are rules you follow and respect, and you are most comfortable when others are doing the same.

This is analogous to argumentation: you need to think about whom you would like to argue with and how you think an argument should proceed. For most of us, it's not too hard to describe the ideal argument partner. Here are the main characteristics you will most likely come up with when describing the *ideal arguer*.

REASONABLE

This would be a person who understands that evidence is important, arguments matter, and things are not true just because she wants them to be, or because she believes in them strongly, or that someone else says they are true.

NOT DOGMATIC

A person who is not dogmatic is someone who is willing, under the right circumstances, to change his mind, who is open to new ideas, and does not see being wrong as a tragic occurrence.

GOOD LISTENER

Someone who wants to understand your position rather than just reiterate her own is a good listener. She is interested in what you are saying and may even offer helpful arguments.

EMPATHETIC

An empathic arguer knows that arguing always involves emotions and intuitions, and they need to be taken into account. She will understand that you are holding a position for a reason, and that reason is meaningful to you. The ideal arguer tries to see things from your point of view.

The ideals then are simply as follows.

1. Be reasonable
2. Do not be dogmatic
3. Listen well
4. Be empathetic

These are the characteristics you would like to see in your audience: You want to be listened to carefully by reasonable, open-minded, and sympathetic people. This can be summarized thus:

GOLDEN RULE OF ARGUMENTATION:
Argue with someone as you would want to be argued with.

This leads you to imagine your ideal audience and enables you to judge an argument by whether or not it would meet the standards of this ideal. When you are judging an argument you are basically asking, is this the kind of argument I want to be presented with? The sort I think is a good argument? This means *you* want to be that kind of audience as well. We do sometimes meet this ideal, as when we are involved in a heuristic inquiry, and sometimes even in persuasion and negotiation. Much depends on the second major component of argument: the context.

Let's stay with the driving example for a bit but move from a typical North American highway to the German Autobahn. On many of those major roads there is no speed limit, just an "advisory" of 130 km/h (80 mph) called a *Richtgeschwindigkeit*. Nonetheless, if you are in the left lane and traveling under 120 mph, you are liable to have horns blaring at you and tailgaters on your back. They are not being rude—you are. The context on the autobahn is different and has different rules, and you only learn them by being there and participating. The difference is akin to being at a family dinner as opposed to a room full of lawyers taking a deposition. Different rules apply.

It should be obvious by now that the rules of argumentation, interactions that take place with people, are highly changeable and highly flexible. Your Critical Thinking training and the rules and methods therein are still important and useful. But, the rules for arguments taking place "on the hoof" are determined by the audience and the context. So doesn't this mean that there really are no rules? Doesn't this mean that it's all just a free-for-all and anything goes? The answer is, No.

First of all, remember something mentioned much earlier: most of the time we argue with people we know and, even more importantly, people with whom we will argue again. When you argue with friends, colleagues, family, co-workers, trades people, professionals, and most of the other people in your life, you know who they are and which set of rules the two of you follow. We mostly argue with familiars, and the opening stage of the discussion was established ages ago. Not only that, if your argument partner is new to you, is perhaps a stranger, but falls into a *category* of person you are familiar with, e.g., a new physician or someone you are introduced to at a party, you assume you will be following the set of rules that applies to that group. If during the course of the interaction things are not proceeding as expected, you may need to return to the opening stage and reexamine the rules.

3.5 COALESCENT ARGUMENT

I want to begin this section with two quotes:

> "Understanding any argumentation, including the intentions involved, must begin as much with the audience as the arguer," says philosopher Christopher Tindale.

> From another quarter, Communication Theorist Dale Hample says, "Focusing attention on people's commitments is enlightening, because it helps us understand why arguments go in various directions, and what sorts of things are arguable once a conversation has begun."

These two categories, Tindale's intentions and Hample's commitments, correspond for our purposes more or less to goals and beliefs, items you have become familiar with already. When we are arguing with familiars the content of these two categories are fairly well known through experience. You know the limits of the goals your co-worker may put before you in the course of a day. If she should want to obtain something more serious or difficult from you than usual, she will preface her comments with something like, "I have a big favor to ask you." This is an indication that she may be going beyond the normal rules or changing her usual goals.

Everyone we are familiar with has a certain ethos, a particular standing, a way in which we regard them, especially with respect to trust and reliability. An individual's ethotic status is, however, subject to change. Your dentist of longstanding may suddenly do work you are not satisfied with, your pub buddy may begin breaking appointments with you, or your co-worker who has always been notoriously unreliable may begin to get everything done on time and be highly cooperative. When changes in behavior like these happen you may adjust the ethotic rating of those people accordingly. These changes take place slowly because it is not easy for us to alter our beliefs about people, their attitudes and goals.

When you deal with familiars you know the rules: You know that your friend Margaríte tends to exaggerate but not to lie; you know your co-worker Sergio has no sense of humor and can't be teased; you know that your manager Gloria always likes to think that every good idea was hers; you know that your doctor Mike always downplays bad news, and so on. The more you know, and the more you are aware of, the better you are able to conduct an argument and achieve agreement. You are entering your audience's world and relying on their values to begin creating an adherence to an outcome you are both happy with. Becoming one with your audience means finding the points of agreement you share so they become the starting point. This means going well beyond the analysis and judgment of an argument presented to you and, rather, understanding it as a whole, as a complete set of values, beliefs and goals.

When arguing with familiars you shouldn't manipulate, dissemble or mislead in any outrageous way because it will come back to bite you—the value of arguing with familiars, your knowledge of their values and beliefs and your awareness of the rules, is also the corrective limit. Because you know all that and because you will argue again, you must protect your own ethotic standing. Reputations rely on the personal history of the familiars, and it is not at all difficult to undermine your standing and lose your credibility. Trust once lost is hard to regain.

Think about it: Amanda shares some information with Jack, swearing him to secrecy. But Jack ends up having dinner with Rachel and Matthew and spills the beans. Rachel, who talks with Amanda all the time, makes it clear she knows the item in question, not realizing she was not supposed to. Amanda says nothing—but what happens to her opinion of Jack? Will she trust him again? Of course, a lot depends on context. We could be talking about something as small as spoiling a surprise party or as monumental as aiding insider trading. Regardless, Jack's ethotic standing will have taken a hit, but the more important the situation, the greater the hit.

While a majority of our argumentative interactions are with familiars, not all of them are. Throughout our lives we are constantly meeting new people and coming into contact with a myriad of folks who cross our paths for one reason or another. Now here's the interesting thing: some of them will *become* familiars. If you imagine they may become familiars, then you know it is important to create a strong ethotic standing for yourself. So, let's break them into two groups, those who you will meet again and those you will not.

I am going to make an assumption about you that I hope is safe. I am going to assume that you are polite and reasonable. This means that when you meet someone who is an un-familiar, you will begin with an attitude that you might also have for a familiar in a similar context. You are not some sort of super eristic who begins each interaction with aggression and hostility. Beginning with a positive attitude is far more likely to engender one in response. As you saw earlier, we know from social psychology that aggression begets aggression, while politeness can be responded to with politeness or aggression. In other words, by being polite at the beginning of an encounter you have a good chance of receiving the same in return, while the opposite, beginning with an aggressive tone will almost surely get you aggression back. Even better, I am going to assume that you are naturally polite and not just adopting an attitude for strategic reasons. Fortunately, this is true of most of us.

What are the sorts of situations in which we meet un-familiars? Continuing in our desire to keep things simple, let's suppose there are two. First is the social/casual, and secondly, the business/commercial. Let's also suppose that this is not necessarily a one-off, and that there's at least a reasonable chance you will meet this person again. This last assumption is crucial, because it means that the ethotic standing created during the first encounter will have lasting effects. In other words, the reputation and image you create will carry over into future meetings. Now here's the trick: most of the time, an un-familiar carries with her or him associations that give you some clues or hints as to who they are, and how you might feel about them. We are, in other words, rarely clueless. So, if you meet someone at a party, you know you have some acquaintances in common; and if you are introduced to someone, you know the person who made the introduction.

Business contexts are no different. If you are going to have a meeting with someone, you will know for whom they work, what their goals likely are, and you may have done some research on them and their company. Companies, after all, have reputations as well. Some are known to be cut-throat, others cooperative, and others self-interested. "Their reputation," as the saying goes, "precedes them." You may also have contacted friends or acquaintances to see if they knew the individual you were to meet. Even when you meet someone about whom you know nothing, your intuitions and instincts come into play. How the person is dressed, whether or not they speak with an accent, where you are, who is with them, all help you create a tentative ethotic standing. So even with unfamiliars you will rarely be without some ethotic clues. You have a wealth of experience, and the myriad clues and tips they each give off will tell you a great deal about your partner.

Once you begin communicating, be it a simple exchange of information or an argument of one sort or another, you will start to identify aspects of your partner's character and incorporate these into your perspective. The rules will emerge through the intricacies of the interaction. You will rely first on the rules you would normally use in a similar interaction with familiars, but the flow of the argument will define and refine those rules. Remember that most people want to be reasonable, and they, like you are aware that there is a good chance of future encounters. What saves the day in both familiar and un-familiar situations is the very simple fact that most people want to be seen as reasonable. Without that, we would get nowhere.

However, it is important to understand two major caveats. First, you have to take the word "most" seriously: there are people who don't care about anyone else, who don't give a farthing for what people think about them. These are the super eristics who run the gamut from just being unpleasant to actually being sociopathic. Fortunately, there are far more reasonable people out there than not. Secondly, the role of familiars is very important here. Even super eristics will *sometimes* care about the feelings and attitudes of their familiars. But you do encounter dictatorial bosses, fanatical polemicists, and people who believe that admitting they're wrong is tantamount to suicide. When that happens all you can do is be as heuristic as possible and hope for the best.

Think of arguing with un-familiars this way: you know the rules, and you assume the person you are arguing with knows them as well. However, what you really don't know is if that person is going to follow them.

3.6 ARGUING WELL

I am going to state that the best way for an argument to end is with agreement. Some may well disagree, but remember that arguments do not always take place in a definite and limited time and place. Many occur and re-occur, "flare up and simmer down" (Willard 1978), but when they do end, as opposed to cease, most of us, most of the time, want that to be an agreement. In different kinds of arguments we have different ideas of what a proper agreement is, but, in the end, it is one sort of agreement or another. In a heuristic inquiry we want to come to an agreement that we have arrived at the best solution or answer to a problem or question; in a persuasion dialogue you want me to agree that the point of view you are presenting is a valuable and worthwhile one; and in a negotiation we want to agree that the arrangement we arrive at is a mutually satisfactory one.

Now agreement by itself is not a sufficient goal of argumentation. Getting agreement by threatening your partner with a gun or by bullying, lying, or other underhanded means, is not the desired goal. It's not desired because on the one hand, such tactics rarely bring lasting agreement, and on the other hand, because—yes you guessed it—this is someone you are likely to argue with again. This is what keeps us reasonable and causes us to want our partners to feel they've been treated fairly. It is the complex dynamic within the argument, the relationship between the participants, context and goals that form the rules. Tindale puts it like this: "Reasonableness arises from the practices of actual reasoners, it is not an abstract code independent of them that they consult for corroboration" (Tindale 2006, 462).

Yet, at the same time, we well know that reasonableness is not always the rule, and there are people who break the rules, and who lie and intimidate. Nonetheless, you should always begin in the same way via the establishment of a basis of agreement. Arguing well means working to find the points of agreement that the arguers share *prior to the divergence of disagreement*. You need to pinpoint the place at which disagreement begins. This means you know what you and your partner agree upon—everything before that—and can look for different ways to move forward from that point. In any case, and in every kind of argument, you need to know where the beginning point of divergence is.

Perelman (1982) talks about "increasing adherence," and if adherence is going to be increased, we must also assume that there was some to start with. Of course, this just makes sense: if you are going to begin arguing with someone you first must find some common ground, someplace from which to launch your dispute or inquiry. Once you have that point you can begin to build on it; you can begin to explore values and beliefs in that place of agreement and move forward. It's like driving and getting lost. One way to deal with that is to go back to where you knew where you were. If you are lost, go back to where you weren't lost.

The necessity for beginning with agreement is critical in every kind of argument. In a heuristic inquiry you typically begin with any number of facts, values and beliefs in common. Then you begin to work toward solutions with those parameters. In a negotiation both parties must approach the bargaining with the idea of succeeding, coming out of a deal feeling satisfied, saving the business, sharing mutual prosperity (or pain,) or arriving at a fair settlement. Without that, what is often referred to as good will, the negotiations will surely break off shortly. In a persuasion dialogue, you also must commence by finding a point on which you both agree. If you do not, then there can be no increase in the adherence of one or the other parties since there was none to begin with.

Having said that, remember that you can find agreement in different areas. Thinking of multi-modal communication (cf. Section 2.2), agreement might be found in the logical arena, the emotional, the visceral or kisceral. Wherever it is, we need it in order to get started, to begin the process of coalescence that will enable us to agree. This puts a great demand on you to listen carefully to your partner's words as well as pay attention to their feelings. You need to be aware of the goals that are in play and be sensitive to alternative ways of reaching them. An important ingredient in pursuing agreement is empathy, and by that I mean understanding the position your dispute partner holds: why does she believe what she does, and how does she see your position as opposing hers? Assuming that you are not at polar opposites, and that there is, somewhere, a light of agreement, you begin to create coalescence from that point.

Understanding a partner's position is complicated by complexity. Positions are typically presented in a verbal form, such as, "I need an extension on my essay," or, "We have to cut benefit costs in this current contract by 26%," or, "Carlton needs to go away to summer camp to increase his independence," or, "If you cared about me, you'd be nice to my mother," and so on. If you think about any one of these assertions and begin to list the beliefs, values, goals and feelings that are likely to be associated with them, the list will very quickly grow quite long. So it is you listening to your argument partner and figuring out which of the multitudinous possibilities are pertinent that enable you to focus in on the most important issues. If you understand the position you are facing, then you are able to examine it for points of agreement, and that means you have potential for building adherence.

In the end there are two sorts of rules for any argument. The first sort are the ones you learned about in Critical Thinking courses and workshops. They include the relationship between premises and conclusions, the sorts of evidence that is relevant, and how much evidence is required to carry a conclusion. Violations of these rules are often captured in mistakes known as fallacies, and arguments that do not meet the standards set by Critical Reasoning rules can be rejected. Even then, Critical Thinking instructs us to use the Principle of Charity to look into and understand the intent of an argument, and try to put it in its best light. The second set of rules arise through the very process of argumentation and are changeable or, at least, flexible, and need to identified *in situ*, that is, within the context and with the specific audience. Here we seek the norms of the ideal arguer but expect that the situation may result in something less than the ideal.

It is important to understand that in a real argument rejecting an argument because it contains an error can be a hasty and wasteful move. When you apply the RSA elements, relevance, sufficiency and acceptability, or whatever analogue is used in your text, you are exposing the workings and strength of your partner's position. This may well lead you to identify errors in reasoning. This is useful because in real argument you can learn a lot about your partner's beliefs, values and goals through a defective argument, so dismissing it may not be a good idea. Yes, we need not accept it as persuasive, but that does not mean it may not convey a good deal of information. The Critical Thinking tools you have will be applied, with experience, in an almost automatic way, as when you learned to drive: you first had to think about everything, but it soon became automatic. Checking for all the RSA components will also become automatic, and little lights will go on to signal difficulties with the argument you are facing.

In this book, you are learning to add to your arsenal, to become comfortable with applying your Critical Thinking skills, and, in addition, those addressed here. So the inclusion of the following will strengthen the skills you already have.

- Be aware of the stage of the argument
- Be aware of the primary mode the argument is in
- Begin by behaving like an ideal arguer
- Begin by assuming your partner is an ideal arguer
- Allow the context and your partner to reveal the rules being followed
- Seek the points of base agreement in order to build adherence
- Always include your partner's goals and respect your partner's values

Arguing with people requires concentrated listening, goodwill, empathy, and flexibility. You are not, after all, arguing by yourself, but with a living breathing partner who will have beliefs, goals and values that almost certainly will not be identical to yours but are as important to them as yours are to you. Arguing with a real person does *not* mean getting what you want; it means finding a point on which you are both as satisfied and content as possible. Even in a heuristic inquiry where "the truth" is being sought, you will both have to agree on how to determine it, how to evaluate the options, and, in the end, just what agreement means. We want our inquiries and arguments to be as heuristic as possible, we want them to be creative and cooperative, we want our partners to be satisfied with the results and look forward to interacting with us again.

In short, we want to be ideal arguers who are communicating with ideal arguers. That doesn't always happen, but it is far more likely if we begin that way than if we don't. To vary an old saying, assume the best, but don't count on it. Arguing is like every other human endeavor, it never travels in a straight line, but, nonetheless, if you pay attention to where you are going, you have a good chance of getting there.

3.7 IN ACTION

You have now acquired a number of new tools that you can use in addition to the ones you got from your Critical Thinking course or workshop. These new tools are designed to help you move within an argument, or more exactly, within an argument$_2$, an interactive, social encounter. In this section you will see how these new tools can be applied in ordinary typical situations.

The Production
Zack is the producer of a training film for a chemical company. The actors are having trouble remembering their lines, but Zack is

opposed to letting them use a teleprompter which will display the script. The director, Michelle, thinks it's necessary, and using it will save several days costs. Actors get paid by the day, while the rest of the crew gets paid a flat fee for the project. They argue.

> Michelle: Zack, I think we should really use the
> teleprompters. All these flubbed lines are costing us time.
> Zack: Hey, these are professional actors, and they're being
> well paid. It's their job to learn their lines.

So we begin: the confrontation stage has been entered, and positions asserted.

1. A BAD START

> M: That's just stupid. We need those teleprompters!

Bad move. Michelle responded with aggression right away—now that's what she'll get back. Watch.

> Z: Well, too bad, I'm the producer and what I say goes.
> M: You can't pull rank on me!

Michelle got aggression right back. Notice now that they are back at the opening stage—what are the limits of their respective powers.

2. A GOOD START

> Z: Hey, these are professional actors, and they're being
> well paid. It's their job to learn their lines.

M: I know that, and you're right—they are professional actors. But this is a different sort of situation.

This is better—Michelle is beginning with agreement.

Z: Why? They have lines and they have to learn them. Period.
M: I know, I know, but a lot of the terminology is very technical—and you're right, they're actors. But it's also right that they're not chemists. These words are all new to them.

Notice how now Michelle is agreeing. She agrees and builds on that. She is also treating Zack like an ideal arguer who will listen to her reasons.

Z: Well, just because the lines are hard doesn't mean they should have it easier.
M: Sure, but we both care about the production first, and the teleprompter would help.

Michelle is appealing to a common goal, and Zack will have a hard time disagreeing with this.

Z: Michelle, the actors earn more on this project than I do or you do, and I expect them to do what they're paid to do.

A light bulb pops over Michelle's head. Maybe there's something going on here other than teleprompters. The argument mode has moved to a more emotional level, and Michelle needs to address Zack's feelings.

M: It's true that their daily rate is higher than ours. But
they're not Hollywood stars. Actors at their level don't
work every day. You're paid a salary by the company, so I'll
bet you make more than any of them annually.

Z: Hmm, I guess that's true.

M: Besides, by slowing down production we need to add
more days, and they'll make even more money.

Z: I hadn't thought of that. All right, go get the teleprompters.

*By realizing that the argument had become an emotional one for Zack,
Michelle was able to address his real feelings. She continued to treat him
as someone who would listen to reason, but allowed the context to show
her what would persuade Zack.*

The Essay

Olivia and James run into each other on campus. It's late in term, and
everyone is stressed with essays and exams. Both of them are fourth
year students, seniors, so there are high expectations in their courses.

James: Hi, Liv, how's it going?

Olivia: Ha. Really crazy. Up to my ears in work and deadlines.

J: Especially that 10 page philosophy essay, I'll bet.

O: Tell me about it. I barely understand half that stuff, let
alone write about it. I honestly don't know where to begin.

J: It's a toughie, and Professor Gilbert's not an easy marker.

O: What about you? Started yet?

J: Ah, well ... Keep it to yourself, but I'm taking a shortcut.

O: A shortcut?

J: Yeah. My sister's boyfriend took this course four years
   ago, and got an A on his essay. So, ...
O: You can't do that!
J: Why not? It's like recycling.

The confrontation stage has been reached.

O: It's nothing like recycling. It's like cheating.
J: Olivia, don't call me a cheater!

An opening stage move—what language is acceptable.

O: Come off it, James. Handing in work that's not yours is
   cheating, pure and simple.
J: I am not a cheater!
O: OK, OK, you're not a cheater. But call it what you will,
   it's against the student code of conduct. Isn't it?

*Olivia decides to allow James his goal of not being a cheater—it may
not be a material point.*

J: All right, I suppose that's true. But I just can't manage
   this paper. It's got me all tied in knots.
O: I understand, James, I really do. But if you get caught
   you'll end up failing, and then you won't even graduate.

James is honestly sharing his feelings, and Olivia responds with empathy.

O [*continuing*]: I know you want to pass, and I believe you
   don't really want to cheat—sorry, shortcut. Have you
   spoken to Prof. Gilbert about it?

J: What can he do?

O: Well, for one thing he can help you focus on a topic and suggest some readings. Can't hurt can it?

J: No, I guess it can't.

O: I mean if you go that route you have a decent chance of passing and little chance of failing. That's a fair trade off, eh?

J: Yeah, it's worth a try.

Olivia was able to alter the context into one where the alternatives were clearer, and the consequences of each more definite. She always treated James as an ideal arguer who would listen and react to her arguments.

Notice how agreeing whenever possible allows you to focus on what is really at issue rather than get bogged down in irrelevant issues. Olivia wants James to realize that there are alternatives to his plan of plagiarism and that the risks of it outweigh the rewards. So why spend time arguing about the definition of cheating.

Binney Cosmetics

For the final example, let me take you back to Binney Cosmetics. You will recall that Binney Cosmetics, BC, is a mid-size family company, privately owned, that is considering outsourcing its helpline. The company is run by two brothers, Chris, the elder by two years, and Paul. Both worked for BC during their summers, but Paul became permanent after he graduated from university. Chris, on the other hand, went to business school and earned an MBA, a Master's of Business Administration. Paul married his high school sweetheart and has four children in school, ranging from High School to 5th grade. Chris is not married, but is in a long term relationship with a woman he met while in business school who lives in New York City. Chris is now Chief Executive Officer and President, and Paul is Chief Operating Officer and Vice-President.

This discussion, not surprisingly, did not take place in one sitting, and it is not possible here to cover the entire process. Instead, you will see snippets that illustrate various principles and ideas.

I. THE BEGINNING

> Chris: Paul, did you look over that report on the outsourcing?
> Paul: I certainly did.
> C: So, what'd you think?
> P: I think you're obviously right—it would save us a lot of money.
> C: So we'll explore it further?
> P: We can explore it as much as you want, but I still think it's a terrible idea.

The confrontation stage has been broached.

> P: [*continuing*] And I'm sure it's just the beginning.
> C: What does that mean?
> P: What it means is that first you'll outsource the call center, then the sales center, and then we'll move the whole plant to Thailand or Mexico or who knows where.
> C: Oh, come on! Doing one thing doesn't mean doing everything.

Chris has recognized Paul's commission of the fallacy of Slippery Slope, and rejected his argument on that grounds.

P: Well, maybe not move the plant, but I'll bet you'll be back at me with reports showing how much we saved and how much more we can save. Can you honestly say that might not happen?

Paul has partially backed off the fallacy, and is making his argument more reasonable. He is also treating Chris like an ideal arguer, and expecting him to be honest.

C: Can't we talk about one thing at a time—like the report in front of you?

Chris is asking for Paul to be more heuristic, to argue more ideally and not change the subject.

C: [*continuing*] Besides, what you call a terrible idea can saved us a heck of a lot of money.

P: There's more to this decision than money, Chris, there's also people.

C: Look, I never said there wouldn't be any collateral damage. I mean yeah, there will be job cuts, and we can do our best to minimize ...

P: [*interrupting*] "Collateral damage!!" You're talking about firing people whose kids go to school with my kids—and some of those call center workers are single mothers.

Chris made the mistake of not taking Paul's values seriously, and this elicits a strong reaction.

C: You're getting emotional, and I don't see ...

P: Yes, I'm getting emotional, and I don't see what's wrong with that. We're part of a community here, and we have a responsibility ...

C: ... to ourselves and our families.

Paul refused to take the accusation of emotionality as justified. Instead, he makes a quick jump back to the opening stage and declares he intends to be emotional.

P: Chris, you're right: we do have a responsibility to ourselves and our families. But Binney Cosmetics has been a family business, and it's not only our families that are involved. Sure, you've been here for a bunch of years, but most weekends you drive to New York to see Natalie. But Kelly and I spend all our time here. We socialize with people here, and we want to be able to hold our heads high and be proud.

C: All right, all right, I didn't realize this was such a big deal to you. But don't you want to make more money?

Chris's move is a good one. He is acknowledging Paul's feelings and not discarding them as irrelevant. Had he done that, the discussion might have gotten bogged down in the opening stage.

P: Of course I want to make more money, but first off, we don't do too badly the way things are, and secondly, maybe we can find other ways of increasing our profits.

C: Okay, kid, let's shelve this for now, and let it be for a while.

P: Yeah, bro, and in the meantime, let's see what other options we have.

Notice that the discussion is not over, but has been put off for another time. In the meanwhile, the brothers have come to realize each other's needs. Paul may have an awareness that Chris feels a need for greater financial resources, and Chris has come to see the emotional component of Paul's position. Had they not been good arguers, the discussion might have devolved into a shouting match, but each was open to the other, and learned from the interaction.

3.8 FINAL WORDS

It's pretty well nigh on impossible to predict how an argument will proceed. The variables are far too numerous: are the arguers aggressives or cooperators, is the argument an inquiry, a persuasion, a negotiation or, like so many, a jumble of all three? Are the arguers schooled? Is there a common familiarity with argument structure, fallacies, and the hallmarks of argument reliability? Is there a desire to be heuristic? A willingness to change? An openness to other ideas and alternative solutions? The list goes on and on.

The most important thing you can do in an argument is to listen and pay attention to what is being said, how it is being said, and what is not being said. You need to apply the tools you have learned here and elsewhere so that they become natural and automatic. Like you saw above, arguing is like driving: When you first begin you have to pay attention to a lot of things, but after a while they become automatic and you hardly think about them at all. Your responses become ingrained: That's why an experienced driver can make an emergency stop, swerve and avoid a tree all at the same time in the flash of a second.

You won't always argue well. I certainly don't. But if the will to do so is there, then at least it can happen, even might happen. If there is no will, then there is no way. So, remember that you want to be an ideal arguer, and, once again, no matter what you might be wrong.

EXERCISES

PART 1

1. Make up an argument$_1$ that can be used in at least two different arguments$_2$. How does the argument$_2$ change the meaning and importance of the argument$_1$?

2. If an argument$_1$ using the same words occurs in two places in an argument$_2$, does it have the same meaning? The same argumentative impact?

3. How many different meanings can you think of that can be given to the word, 'yes,' the word, 'great'? What makes the meaning change?

4. With a partner: A finds a statement that is irrefutable. B finds an argument that questions it. Can you find anything that is not a tautology, i.e., a logical truth or a definition, that cannot be questioned?

5. In the TV show *Star Trek*, the character Mr. Spock was of Vulcan descent. This meant that he did not express or react to human emotion. With whom would you rather have an argument, the Vulcan Mr. Spock or the human Captain Kirk? Why?

6. Would your choice in 1.5 be consistent, or would it vary according to the topic or context?

7. Describe the rules you use when arguing with a friend. Now describe the rules when arguing with a manager or teacher or other person in authority. What are the differences? Are they always the same? Can they change over time?

8. Using the example of Binney Cosmetics (p. 112), make a list of the distinct arguments that might arise in the course of a discussion. Compare your list to a partner's. What do the differences in the lists tell you?

9. Ralph and Tony are arguing about the importance of careful language in US legal documents. Ralph points out that in South Africa there are formal rules for sentence construction. Which of the following indicates a change of stage?
   1. Tony says, who cares about that?
   2. Tony says, that's a myth.
   3. Tony says, Oh, the heck with it, and storms away.

10. Paul and Chris, sons of the founder of Binney Cosmetics, are discussing the outsourcing issue mentioned above (p. 112). They want to conduct a heuristic inquiry to the best of their ability. With a partner, assume their roles and do the following.
   1. List all items that might be contentious.
   2. Select two, and under each item list all arguments pro and con by both first finding pro and then both finding con arguments. How difficult is this? Can you feel yourself drawn to one position or another?

For use in 1.11–1.13, you and a partner have to write a report on having a negotiation. This must include:
   1. The subject

2. *Researching the material*
3. *Creating a first draft*
4. *Reviewing the draft for*
   a. *Content*
   b. *Spelling*
   c. *Grammar*
5. *Following the revision to create a second draft*

11. Using the above, decide which of items 1-5 you prefer to do. Have a negotiation designed to make sure you do the parts you want to and only the parts you want to. Be eristic, that is, try to get what you want without caring about your partner's goals or feelings.

12. Using the same report, undertake a heuristic inquiry. Begin by being clear on what you want and why. Explain, in turns, why you believe you can do the best report by undertaking particular parts.

13. Now, write the report about the process.

14. While increasing the heuristic level with each turn, have a persuasion dialogue with your partner on each of the following. Remember to begin with an eristic outlook.
   a. 1 + 1 does not always equal 2.
   b. Women ought to do more housework than men.
   c. Older people are wiser than younger people.
   d. Studying argumentation is a waste of time.

15. Go back now to the last exercise and re-examine your process in b-d. Where, if anywhere, was there a dialogue switch? How did it happen? How did it impact the negotiation?

PART 2

1. Make a list of familiars. Who are the people with whom you regularly have discussions? Rank the list in order of frequency.

2. Using the list from 2.1, describe the different contexts in which these dialogues take place. How does the context impact the discussion?

3. With reference to the example Peter's Camp (p. 57), you and your partner separately make lists of alternatives regarding Peter's summer that might satisfy Kelly. When you are done, compare them. Which of these would also satisfy Natalie?

4. You and your partner adopt the roles of Kelly and Natalie. Take some small pieces of paper, and on each write the words 'logical,' 'emotional,' 'visceral,' and 'kisceral,' until you have four of each. Fold them and put them in a container. Again using Peter's Camp and relying on the lists you came up with in 2.3 make an argument in the mode you select from the container. Whichever partner is receiving the argument should record its content, but do not reveal it in this exercise.

   What differences occur? Did you find that a particular mode was more comfortable to you when making arguments? When receiving them?

5. Exchange the notes you made in 2.4, does the description of your argument match your intent? Discuss the differences and see if you can point to why the record does not match the message.

6. Staying with the results of 2.3, do the following. Take each of the alternatives, and with your partner, list aspects of it that you can agree with.

7. Use the example, The Audit (p. 68), with one partner being the Vice President, VP, and the other being the Plant Manager, PM. Continue the argument by changing your degrees of aggressivity and agreeableness, and alter your levels of argumentativeness. Note what happens, and especially how the argument becomes more or less difficult and enjoyable.

8. In this exercise you'll play with gender stereotypes. One of you will adopt the masculine role and one the feminine. The feminine will be an argument avoider, a conflict avoider, and eager to maintain a positive relationship. The masculine will be more aggressive, concerned about hierarchy, and keen to be the one to solve the problem. Using The Audit again, play with these roles. What differences arise? Finally, do you know people who meet these stereotypes?

PART 3

1. Pretend you don't know each other. You are going to have an argument about eating meat. In each of the following cases, notice how the information comes out and how the subsequent argument behaves differently. What do you learn about your partner? How do the different reasons give you information about the person you are communicating with? (Make notes, you will be referring to these arguments again.)

    a. In this argument one of you is morally opposed to eating meat.

    b. Next, one of you has religious reasons.

    c. Now, one of you has medical reasons for not eating meat.

2. Selecting one of the scenarios in 3.1, have a discussion where one of you is unwilling to reveal the reason. How is it different? Do you notice any frustration?

3. Think of the people you know. Which of them is the most sensitive? Which the least? How does this make them different? Which one seems to communicate better? Why?

4. Make a list of 15 beliefs you hold ranging from the very strongest, e.g., the light on my desk is on, to the least tightly held, e.g., a week Tuesday I'm getting my nails done. Now go back through the list and re-think which could—*just could*—conceivably be wrong. Discuss with a partner those listed as absolutely necessary.

5. One of the ways in which workers conducting a protest sometimes make their point is using a tactic called "work to rule." What is this, and what can it tell us about the difference between the way rules say the world should work and the way it really does? Is there only one way to work to rule?

6. Reflect on the arguments in 3.1 and 3.2. What rules were followed, and what rules were violated. How different were the rules used in 3.1 from 3.2?

7. Consider having an argument about deadlines and how important they are. These are the different cases. Notice if and how the rules differ in each case.
   a. You are a student having this argument with your mother.
   b. You are a manager having this argument with one of your staff.
   c. You are a friend whose friend promised to make reservations.

8. With a partner make a list of 10 outrageous statements, on the order of, "Dogs should be allowed to marry." Now one of you take that position, and the other find aspects of it that you can agree with.

9. Write a list of the characteristics of your ideal argument partner. Compare it to others. Which traits are in everyone's? Which are unique?

10. This exercise requires three people. With a partner and an observer, pick a topic. You might choose,
   a. The Academy Awards are a useless waste of time.
   b. Everyone should have a three month paid vacation every five years.
   c. University education should be free.

Paying attention to your list characteristics, slowly conduct an argument, but the observer is permitted to stop you any time you violate one of the traits you listed.

11. This exercise will use the case study The Production on p. 107. If enacted, it needs three people, but can also be done individually as a written exercise. Use the case, but stop at Michelle's last line, before Zack agrees. So their conversation ends with:

M: Besides, by slowing down production we need to add more days, and they'll make even more money.

Now comes the change: You are one of the actors, and you just happen along.

M [*whispers to Zack*]: Shh!

You: Hi, what's doing?

M: Actually we were discussing teleprompters. [*Michelle summarizes the discussion for you.*]

A. You want the teleprompters because you feel the technical vocabulary is ruining the performances, and you are concerned with the results. How would you continue the argument?

B. You have no work lined up following this gig, so you are happy for it to go on as long as it can. You can be eristic.

What differences do you notice as a result of the change in goals? How do the two arguments differ? Write up your thoughts.

12. This exercise requires two people. Referring to Binney Cosmetics on p. 112, imagine that you and your partner are Kelly, Paul's wife, and Natalie, Chris's fiancée. Kelly enjoys her life in their community, but Natalie is not ready to settle down and loves the New York lifestyle. Besides, she has her own career there as a magazine production designer. Refresh your memory of gender differences in argumentation in Section 2.5 and have the argument between yourselves.

A. In this case you are each trying to get what you want. It is a persuasion dialogue, and can range from heuristic to eristic.

B. In this case you are trying hard to maintain a heuristic inquiry. Can you reach a resolution?

Each partner should write a summary of the discussion. How did the two parts differ? How did the results differ?

FURTHER READING

There are many books written on Critical Thinking and Informal Logic, and most of them are useful. The books that I list here are more oriented to Argumentation Theory, though some traditional ones are included for rounding out.

1. EASIEST

Battersby, Mark. 2010. *Is that a fact?* Peterborough, ON: Broadview.

Bickenbach, Jerome Edmund, and Jacqueline MacGregor Davies. 1997. *Good reasons for better arguments: an introduction to the skills and values of critical thinking.* Peterborough, ON: Broadview.

Gilbert, Michael A. 2008. *How to win an argument: surefire strategies for getting your point across.* 3rd ed. Lanham, MD: UP of America. Original edition, 1979.

Govier, Trudy. 2001. *A practical study of argument.* Belmont, CA: Wadsworth Thomson Learning. Original edition, 1985.

Groarke, Leo, and Christopher W. Tindale. 2003. *Good reasoning matters!: a constructive approach to critical thinking.* Toronto; New York: Oxford UP.

Saindon, Jean Emmett, and Peter John Krek. 2014. *Critical thinking: argument and argumentation.* 2nd ed. Toronto: Nelson Education.

Tindale, Christopher W. 2004. *Rhetorical argumentation: principles of theory and practice*. Thousand Oaks, CA: Sage.

2. MORE DIFFICULT

Avtgis, Theodore A., and Andrew S. Rancer. 2010. *Arguments, aggression, and conflict: new directions in theory and research*. New York: Routledge.

Eemeren, Frans van, and R. Grootendorst. 1992. *Argumentation, communication, and fallacies: a pragma-dialectical perspective*. Hillsdale, NJ: L. Erlbaum.

———. 2004. *A systematic theory of argumentation: the pragma-dialectical approach*. New York: Cambridge UP.

———, R. Grootendorst, and A.F. Snoeck Henkemans. 1996. *Fundamentals of argumentation theory: a handbook of historical backgrounds and contemporary developments*. Mahwah, NJ: L. Erlbaum.

Gilbert, Michael A. 1997. *Coalescent argumentation*. Mahwah, NJ: Routledge.

Hamblin, Charles L. 1970. *Fallacies*. London: Methuen.

Hample, Dale. 2005. *Arguing: exchanging reasons face to face*. Mahwah, NJ: L. Erlbaum.

Johnson, Ralph H. 2000. *Manifest rationality: a pragmatic theory of argument*. Mahwah, NJ; London: L. Erlbaum.

Perelman, Chaim. 1982. *The realm of rhetoric*. Notre Dame, IN: U of Notre Dame P.

Rancer, Andrew S., and Theodore A. Avtgis. 2006. *Argumentative and aggressive communication: theory, research, and application*. Thousand Oaks, CA: Sage.

Tindale, Christopher W. 1999. *Acts of arguing: a rhetorical model of argument*. Albany, NY: State U of New York P.

Walton, Douglas. 1998. *The new dialectic: conversational contexts of argument*. Toronto: U of Toronto P.

Willard, Charles A. 1989. *A theory of argumentation*. Tuscaloosa: U of Alabama P.

3. JOURNALS

The top journals in the field of argumentation include the following:

Argumentation

Argumentation and Advocacy

Informal Logic online:
<http://ojs.uwindsor.ca/ojs/leddy/ index.php/informal_logic>

Philosophy & Rhetoric

BIBLIOGRAPHY

Brockriede, Wayne. 1972. "Arguers as Lovers." *Philosophy & Rhetoric* 5 (1): 1-11.

Damasio, Antonio R. 1994. *Descartes' error: emotion, reason, and the human brain*. New York: G.P. Putnam.

DNA. 2012. "Train." In *Collins English Dictionary—Complete & Unabridged 10th Edition*, ed Dictionary.com. <http://dictionary.reference.com/browse/train>: HarperCollins Publishers (accessed July 19, 2012).

Edwards, Keith E., and Susan R. Jones. 2009. "Putting My Man Face On": A Grounded Theory of College Men's Gender Identity Development." *Journal of College Student Development* 50 (2): 210-28.

Eemeren, Frans van, R. Grootendorst, and A.F. Snoeck Henkemans. 1996. *Fundamentals of argumentation theory: a handbook of historical backgrounds and contemporary developments*. Mahwah, NJ: L. Erlbaum.

Fisher, R., and W. Ury. 1981. *Getting to yes: negotiating agreement without giving in*. Boston: Houghton Mifflin.

Frodi, A., J. Macaulay, and P.R. Thome. 1977. "Are Women Always Less Aggressive than Men?" *Psychological Bulletin* 84 (4): 634-60.

Gilbert, Michael A. 1994. "What Is an Emotional Argument, or, Why Do Argumentation Theorists Argue with their Mates?" Proceedings of the Third Conference of the International Society for the Study of Argumentation, Amsterdam, NL, 1995.

———. 1997. *Coalescent argumentation*. Mahwah, NJ: Routledge.

———. 2001. "Emotional Messages." *Argumentation* 15 (3): 239-49.

———. 2007. "Natural Normativity: Argumentation Theory as an Engaged Discipline." *Informal Logic* 27 (2): 149-61.

———. 2008. *How to win an argument: surefire strategies for getting your point across*. 3rd ed. Lanham, MD: UP of America. Original edition, 1979.

Habermas, Jurgen. 1990. *Moral consciousness and communicative action*. Translated by Christian Lenhardt and Shierry Weber Nicholsen. Cambridge, MA: MIT P.

Hample, Dale. 2007. "The Arguers." *Informal Logic* 27 (2): 163–78.

———, and Ioana A. Cionea. 2010. "Taking Conflict Personally and Its Connections with Aggression." In *Arguments, aggression, and conflict: new directions in theory and research*, edited by Theodore A. Avtgis and Andrew S. Rancer, 372-87. New York: Routledge.

Infante, Daniel A., A.S. Rancer, and F.F. Jordan. 1996. "Affirming and Nonaffirming Style, Dyad Sex, and the Perception of Argumentation and Verbal Aggression in an Interpersonal Dispute." *Human Communication Research* 22 (3): 315-34.

Johnson, Ralph H. 2000. *Manifest rationality: a pragmatic theory of argument.* Mahwah, NJ; London: Lawrence Erlbaum Associates.

Lakoff, R.T. 1990. *Talking power: the politics of language in our lives.* New York: Basic Books.

Maltz, Daniel, and Ruth Borker. 1982. "A Cultural Approach to Male-Female Communication." In *Language and social identity*, edited by J.J. Gumperz. Cambridge, Cambridgeshire; New York: Cambridge UP.

O'Keefe, Daniel J. 1977. "Two Concepts of Argument." *JAFA: Journal of the American Forensic Association* 13 (3): 121-28.

Perelman, Chaim. 1982. *The realm of rhetoric*. Notre Dame, IN: U of Notre Dame P.

———, and Lucie Olbrechts-Tyteca. 1969. *The new rhetoric: a treatise on argumentation*. Translated by John Wilkinson and Purcell Weaver. Notre Dame [IN]: U of Notre Dame P. Original edition, 1958 (in French).

Popper, K.R. 1979. *Objective knowledge: an evolutionary approach*. Oxford: Clarendon Press.

Rancer, Andrew S., and Theodore A. Avtgis. 2006. *Argumentative and aggressive communication: theory, research, and application*. Thousand Oaks, CA: Sage.

Richmond, Virginia P., and James C. McCroskey. 2010. "Tolerance for Disagreement." In *Arguments, aggression, and conflict: new directions in theory and research*, edited by Theodore A. Avtgis and Andrew S. Rancer, 359-371. New York: Routledge.

Sosa, David. 2006. "Scepticism about Intuition." *Philosophy: The Journal of the Royal Institute of Philosophy* 81 (318): 633-47.

Tannen, Deborah. 1990. *You just don't understand: women and men in conversation*. New York: Morrow.

Tindale, Christopher W. 1999. *Acts of arguing: a rhetorical model of argument*. Albany, NY: State U of New York P.

———. 2004. *Rhetorical argumentation: principles of theory and practice*. Thousand Oaks, CA: Sage.

———. 2006. "Constrained Maneuvering: Rhetoric as a Rational Enterprise." *Argumentation* 20 (4): 447-66.

Trapp, R., and N. Huff. 1985. "A Model of Serial Argument in Interpersonal Relationships." *JAFA: Journal of the American Forensic Association* 22 (1).

Walton, Douglas. 1998. *The new dialectic: conversational contexts of argument.* Toronto: U of Toronto P.

———, and Eric C.W. Krabbe. 1995. *Commitment in dialogue: basic concepts of interpersonal reasoning.* Albany: State U of New York P.

Wenzel, Joseph. 1979. "Perspectives on Argument." Summer Conference on Argumentation.

Willard, Charles A. 1978. "A Reformulation of the Concept of Argument: The Constructivist/Interactionist Foundations of a Sociology of Argument." *Journal of the American Forensic Association* 14: 121-40.

———. 1989. *A theory of argumentation.* Tuscaloosa: U of Alabama P.

INDEX

from the publisher

A name never says it all, but the word "broadview" expresses a good deal of the philosophy behind our company. We are open to a broad range of academic approaches and political viewpoints. We pay attention to the broad impact book publishing and book printing has in the wider world; we began using recycled stock more than a decade ago, and for some years now we have used 100% recycled paper for most titles. As a Canadian-based company we naturally publish a number of titles with a Canadian emphasis, but our publishing program overall is internationally oriented and broad-ranging. Our individual titles often appeal to a broad readership too; many are of interest as much to general readers as to academics and students.

Founded in 1985, Broadview remains a fully independent company owned by its shareholders—not an imprint or subsidiary of a larger multinational.

If you would like to find out more about Broadview and about the books we publish, please visit us at **www.broadviewpress.com**. And if you'd like to place an order through the site, we'd like to show our appreciation by extending a special discount to you: by entering the code below you will receive a 20% discount on purchases made through the Broadview website.

Discount code: **broadview20%**

Thank you for choosing Broadview.

Please note: this offer applies only to sales of bound books within the United States or Canada.

The interior of this book is printed on 100% recycled paper.

   BIO GAS
ENERGY